1

FROM PARADOR TO PARADOR SPAIN

TOURIST PARADORES

ISBN: 84-85983-14-9
Volume 1: 84-85983-15-7
Volume 2: 84-85983-16-5
Depósito Legal: B. 22.219-83

Printed in Spain, by LUNA WENNBERG EDITORES 1983
General Mitre, 191-193 - BARCELONA - Tel. (93) 212 42 08
Núñez de Balboa, 115 - MADRID - Tel. (91) 262 80 46

ADMINISTRACIÓN TURÍSTICA ESPAÑOLA
Agustín de Bethencourt, 25, 2.º
Tels. (91) 234 57 49 - 234 58 37 - 234 61 03
MADRID-3 Telex: 46865 RRPP

1

FROM PARADOR TO PARADOR SPAIN

TOURIST PARADORES

WRITTEN BY

Pedro Altares
Luis María Ansón
José María de Areilza
J.J. Armas Marcelo
Jaime de Armiñán
Juan Benet
Jaime del Burgo
José Manuel Caballero Bonald
Joaquín Calvo Sotelo
A.M. Campoy
Luis Carandell
J.L. Castillo Puche
Luis de Castresana
José María Castroviejo
Camilo José Cela
Oscar Collazos
Juan Cruz Ruiz
Miguel Delibes
Gerardo Fernández Albor
Jesús Fernández Santos
Manuel Fraga Iribarne
Joan Fuster
José García Nieto
Francisco García Pavón
Domingo García Sabell
Antonio Garrigues y Díaz Cañabate
José María Gironella
Félix Grande
Alfonso Grosso
Pedro de Lorenzo
Torcuato Luca de Tena
Nestor Luján
Julián Marías
Carmen Martín Gaite
Carlos Murciano
Francisco Nieva
Carmen Nonell
Domingo Pérez Minik
Manuel Pombo Angulo
Claudio Rodríguez
Luis Rosales
Alejandro Royo-Villanova
Fernando Sánchez Dragó
Víctor de la Serna
Francisco Umbral
Jesús Vasallo
Manuel Vicent
Alonso Zamora Vicente

INTRODUCTION

The fact that there are 87 National Paradores set up from one end of Spain to the other, each one with its own history and all ensconced in highly diverse areas of touristic appeal, is a detail which should not escape the curiosity of Spaniards and foreigners alike. On account of this, the need arose to present a book like this one, in which the practical information is as thorough as the extremely personal style which each writer has given his or her chosen Parador.

By glancing over the list of authors it can be seen that each of them is a well-known and up-to-date Spanish writer versed – through his works and origins – in the culture of the chosen area or region. From historical explanations (which would not be enough) to cultural ones, and without skipping over points of interest such as gastronomy and local customs, each one is a journey both inside and outside the Parador. In most cases they are short and splendid pieces of literature.

How should all of this valuable material be put in order? In the first place, it was necessary to make a selection of the Paradores and, as a result, of the existing texts, owing to the technical possibilities of the book. It would have been excessive if they had been taken in their entirety and accompanied by abundant photographic material.

One method was therefore chosen from among all the possibilities: preparing a detailed map, marking the geographical position of each Parador and excluding those located in what we might call "highly saturated areas". We ran the risk of excluding some of unquestioned notability; it was, however, an unavoidable hazard. A more voluminous production would have been editorially impractical on account of its high cost and a much lower likelihood of national and international exposure.

In the second place, it was essential to eschew a mere miscellany of texts which would have appeared as a barely enjoyable literary anthology as well as a somewhat conventional editorial solution. The idea then arose of drawing up a more or less logical route which would cover all or almost all of Spain from an imaginary starting-point. As far as possible, the itinerary was worked out to follow a route roughly in accordance with the trips which a traveller might make if willing either to stay overnight at each Parador or at least get to know all of them. Another equally practical and attractive aid, apart from the map which accompanies this book, was envisioned: including a lengthier text somewhat like a traveller's diary which would connect all the other writings included in these volumes. Our compilation of texts would have fallen into tediousness if it were not for this.

Being conceived as an ordered and concise narrative, the *Traveller's Notes* link the itinerary with each of the individual essays. It is obvious that this is but one of the possible itineraries and that the selection of the adventure undertaken by its author is imaginary and hypothetical.

At whom is this ambitious work, conceived as a vast informative panel and, at the same time, an aesthetic production, aimed? Undoubtedly, at everyone who wishes to discover the marvels of the National Paradores and the scenic geography of Spain. There could be no better way to achieve this objective than by translating the literary material into the main European languages; this is what we have done, while giving thought to the ever more urgent need to promote abroad one of the highest accomplishments in our tourist industry and culture.

In addition to the literature, the reader will find a map based on a close study of the geographical areas offered to the traveller as well as sufficient photographs of each Parador and its surroundings. Details of the interiors of these splendid buildings have been added to the purely architectural assessment as well as views of their furnishings and, in some cases, panoramas of the cities where they are located.

If informing the world about our touristic offer is as important as promoting it, then equally important is the artistic conception of this offer. We believe that both objectives have been fulfilled through this presentation. We have tried to go beyond a simple informative brochure, to enhance the merits and value of the Paradores both individually and as a whole. And to view them as a monumental interconnection of the extraordinarily rich, varied and polymorphic Spanish geography. *From Parador to Parador: Spain* manages to fill an informative vacuum. And, what is more, it is an invaluable work thanks to the writers brought together in it. We have no doubt of the interest which this book will arouse, seeing that up to now no other publication of this magnitude has been attempted.

THE PARADORES OF TOURISM

THE ORIGINS OF THE NETWORK

In the year 1926, when the Marqués de la Vega Inclán (who can indubitably be considered the first promotor of Spanish tourism) was the Royal Commissioner for Tourism, King Alfonso XIII personally selected the location of the National Parador of Gredos, the first of a series of hotels which was to form the present-day network of Paradores.
Construction commenced in May and continued throughout the two following years until it was successfully terminated in October 1928, subsequently being officially inaugurated on the 9th of the same month, with the King himself presiding over the ceremonies.

THE PURPOSE OF THE NETWORK

Two other no less significant objectives were soon joined to the original idea of opening up zones of unquestionable scenic beauty with the opportunity of hunting and fishing: restoring and setting up historic monuments on the point of being lost forever, and the chance of providing the motorist with a place of rest to regain his energy from the journeys made along the main routes; these latter were located at the final points of the limited stages which could be reached with the automotive technology available.

For the first of these two objectives there thus appeared hotels like the National Parador of Oropesa, which was set up in the palace of the Duke of Frías, the one in Ubeda in the ancient palace of the High Constable Dávalos, the one in Ciudad Rodrigo in the castle of Enrique II of Trastámara, that of Mérida in the convent of the Order of St. Clare, the hostería of Alcalá de Henares in a wing of the university of Alcalá, which was founded by Cardinal Cisneros, and so forth.
As for the motorway establishments – the forerunners of our modern motels – a number of twelve was planned in the beginning; all have an adequate supply of services and even provide small petrol stations amongst their installations.
As time went by, and as the preferences of our visitors became more and more exacting, the State did not turn a blind eye to the new trends and decided to expand its chain of establishments by promoting new tourist areas in which private enterprise would not invest on account of uncertain profitability. It was also resolved to support the use of the hotel-trade names in disuse but with deeply-rooted popular traditions such as *Paradores* (Hotels), *Posadas* (Inns), *Hosterías* (Restaurants), etc., as well as bringing the excellent qualities of the Spanish cuisine to light at the same time.

It was noted during the tourist explosion which began in the sixties that the "shortcomings" with regard to the classes and prices set by private hotels needed to be somewhat rectified, so a new objective was introduced: placing establishments in the areas where these irregularities had been most evident.

When all of these goals had been reached - or, at least, had the groundwork laid for them to be carried out - a final effort was made to try to complete the state hotel network with an ambitious project; namely, making sure that each and every Spanish province had at least one establishment to aid not only their tourist development but also, even if only on a small scale, improve their social needs by providing new job opportunities, as well as their economies by the likelihood of increasing the demand of services and goods from small businesses. All this was done while walking the difficult tightrope of respecting the interests of private enterprise without ever commercially competing with it.

In order to achieve these objectives, the mission which these establishments had to fulfil, as well as their merit from a touristic, geographical and recreational viewpoint, was taken into consideration.

As regards the first point, the buildings of the network were divided into *Paradores, Albergues, Hosterías* and *Refugios* upon giving thought to the rôle they had to play and the special characteristics of the guests who would be using their services.

Paradores are designed for long stays in places which are ideal for relaxation or strategically located to get to know the surroundings.

Motorway Albergues are situated alongside the main transport routes and offer stays limited to 48 hours - due to their general public usefulness - for travellers using their own means of transport to tour the country.

Refugios are mountain shelters set up to take in hikers and sportsmen during their excursions or to serve them as operational bases.

Hosterías have the mission of presenting the Spanish gastronomic virtues in the special style of the regions in which they are located. They have no bedrooms.

With the passing of the years, and in view of the changes that have occurred in the tourism framework as well as the mentality of the traveller who stays at a hotel, these distinctions have in practice been gradually fading away and we can now say that apart from the *Hosterías* - as their name indicates, they continue to offer only restaurant services - all of the establishments operate in a similar fashion.

We are now going to speak about the touristic, geographical and recreational situation which we mentioned earlier. It has often been said that Spain is like a small-scale continent. Its 3,500 kilometres of coastline, its seven great mountain chains and its islands offer landscapes and sites of extreme beauty, environmental tranquility and highly dissimilar climates. Being aware of the importance of these phenomena, the Network owns establishments in such areas as the Mediterranean coast (the Paradores of Aiguablava on the Costa Brava, Tortosa on the Costa Dorada, Jávea, Malaga and Torremolinos on the Costa del Sol), Cadiz, Mazagón and Ayamonte on the South Atlantic, Fuenterrabía, Santillana, Gijón and Ribadeo on the Cantabrian Corniche, as well as Cambados, Pontevedra, Bayona and Tuy along the Rías Bajas in Galicia.

An attempt to promote the flow of tourists to the mountains - apart from only sportsmen - has been made by constructing Paradores such as Bielsa, Artíes and Viella in the Pyrenees. Fuente Dé and Pajares in the Cantabrian Cordillera, Gredos in the Central Massif and Sierra Nevada, with an altitude of 2,500 metres above sea-level, in the Andalusian mountain range.

The charm of our islands could not help but be part of this geographic consideration. The Network has covered practically all of the possibilities on the Canaries: from the almost inaccessible volcanic landscapes of Teide and Tejeda on Tenerife and Gran Canaria respectively to the deserts of Fuerteventura, without leaving out the orchards of La Palma and Gomera Islands.

Sports and recreations form the other sector which the Network tries to serve with its establishments by giving access to water sports, skiing, hunting, fishing, golf and tennis. Special emphasis is given to big-game hunting in Cazorla, Fuente Dé, Gredos, Fuentes Carrionas and Ojén, as well as salmon and trout fishing in Ribadeo and Gredos.

Golf, a select sport needing special characteristics as regards installations, is provided on the Network's private courses located at the Paradores of El Saler and Torremolinos.

And, last but not least, there are many establishments which have their own tennis courts to practise on.

The numbers on the map correspond to each parador as well as the photograph and text numbers for an easier location of each parador's pictures and stories. The symbol △ signify that there is a Parador the symbol • signify that there are not photographs

△ 1 Parador del Valle de Arán. Viella. (Lérida).

△ 4 Parador de Ordesa. (Huesca.)

△ 6 Parador "Monte Perdido". Bielsa. (Huesca).

△ 10 Parador "Don Gaspar de Portolá". Arties. (Lérida).

△ 15 Parador de Seo de Urgel. Seo de Urgel. (Lérida).

△ 17 Parador "Duques de Cardona". Cardona. (Barcelona).

△ 20 Parador de Vich. Vich. (Barcelona).

△ 23 Parador "Costa Brava". Aiguablava. (Gerona).

△ 26 Parador "Castillo de la Zuda". Tortosa. (Tarragona).

△ 28 Parador "Costa del Azahar". Benicarló. (Castellón).

△ 30 Parador "La Concordia". Alcañiz. (Teruel).

△ 32 Parador de Teruel. Teruel.

△ 35 Parador "Luis Vives". El Saler. (Valencia).

△ 37 Parador "Marqués de Villena". Alarcón. (Cuenca).

△ 40 Parador "La Mancha". Albacete.

△ 43 Parador "Costa Blanca". Jávea. (Alicante).

△ 47 Parador Puerto Lumbreras. Puerto Lumbreras. (Murcia).

△ 48 Parador "Reyes Católicos". Mojacar. (Almería).

△ 52 Parador "El Adelantado". Cazorla. (Jaén).

△ 57 Parador "Condestable Dávalos". Ubeda. (Jaén).

△• A Parador de Bailén. (Jaén).

△• B Parador de Manzanares. Manzanares. (Ciudad Real).

△ 64 Parador de Almagro. Almagro. (Ciudad Real).

△ 66 Parador "Castillo de Santa Catalina". Jaén.

△ 70 Parador "La Arruzafa". Cordova.

△ 72 Parador "San Francisco". Granada.

△ 76 Parador de Sierra Nevada. Monachil. (Granada).

△ 79 Parador de Nerja. Nerja. (Málaga).

△ 83 Parador de Antequera. Málaga.

△ 86 Parador de "Juanar". Ojén. (Málaga).

△ 88 Parador "Del Golf". Torremolinos. (Málaga).

△ 90 Parador de "Gibralfaro". Málaga.

△ 94 Parador "Don Pedro de Estopiñán". Melilla.

△ 97 Parador de las Cañadas del Teide. (Tenerife).

△ 100 Parador "Conde de la Gomera". (La Gomera).

△ 104 Parador de Santa Cruz de la Palma. (Isla de la Palma).

△ 106 Parador de Hierro. (Hierro).

△ 110 Parador "Cruz de Tejeda". Cruz de Tejeda. (Gran Canaria).

△ 114 Parador "Fuerteventura". Puerto del Rosario. (Fuerteventura).

△ 122 Parador de Cádiz.

△ 127 Parador "Casa del Corregidor". Arcos de la Frontera. (Cádiz).

△ 131 Parador "Alcázar del Rey don Pedro". Carmona. (Seville).

△ 134 Parador "Cristóbal Colón". Mazagón-Moguer. (Huelva).

△ 139 Parador "Costa de la Luz". Ayamonte. (Huelva).

△ 142 Parador "Hernán Cortés". Zafra. (Badajoz).

△ 146 Parador "Vía de la Plata". Mérida. (Badajoz).

△ 153 Hostería "El Comendador". Cáceres.

△ 156 Parador "Zurbarán". Guadalupe. (Cáceres).

△ 159 Parador "Virrey Toledo". Oropesa. (Toledo).

△ 161 Parador "Carlos V". Jarandilla de la Vera. (Cáceres).

△ 165 Parador de Gredos. Navarredonda. (Ávila).

△ 168 Parador "Enrique II". Ciudad Rodrigo. (Salamanca).

△ 171 Parador de Salamanca. Salamanca.

△ 173 Parador "Condes de Alba y Aliste". Zamora.

△ 177 Parador de Tordesillas. Tordesillas. (Valladolid)

△ 178 Parador "Fernando II de León". Benavente. (Zamora).

△ 182 Parador "Monterrey". Verín. (Orense).

△ 184 Parador "San Telmo". Tuy. (Pontevedra).

△ 186 Parador "Conde de Gondomar". Bayona. (Pontevedra).

△ 190 Parador "Casa del Barón". Pontevedra.

△ 194 Parador "Del Albariño". Cambados. (Pontevedra).

△ 201 Parador de El Ferrol. El Ferrol. (Coruña).

△ 203 Parador "Condes de Villalba". Villalba. (Lugo).

△ 205 Parador de Ribadeo. Ribadeo. (Lugo).

△ 211 Parador de Villafranca del Bierzo. Villafranca del Bierzo. (León).

△ 213 Parador "Puerto de Pajares". Pajares. (Oviedo).

△ 219 Parador "Molino Viejo". Gijón. (Oviedo).

△ 220 Parador "Río Deva". Fuente Dé. (Santander).

△ 225 Parador "Gil Blas". Santillana del Mar. (Santander).

△ 232 Parador "Fuentes Carrionas". Cervera de Pisuerga. (Palencia).

△ 237 Parador "Pintor Zuloaga". Pedraza. (Segovia).

△ 240 Parador de Segovia. Segovia.

△ 243 Parador de Villacastín. Villacastín. (Segovia).

△ 246 Parador "Raimundo de Borgoña". Ávila.

△ 249 Parador "Conde de Orgaz". Toledo.

△ 256 Parador de Chinchón. (Madrid).

△ 258 Hostería "Del Estudiante". Alcalá de Henares. (Madrid).

△ 260 Parador "Castillo de Sigüenza". Sigüenza. (Guadalajara).

△● C Parador de Santa María de Huerta. Santa María de Huerta. (Soria).

△ 269 Parador "Antonio Machado". Soria.

△ 271 Parador de Santo Domingo de la Calzada. Santo Domingo de la Calzada. (Rioja).

△ 273 Parador "Marco Fabio Quintiliano". Calahorra. (Rioja).

△ 276 Parador de Argómaniz. Argómaniz. (Álava).

△ 279 Parador "Príncipe de Viana". Olite. (Navarra).

△ 284 Parador "Fernando de Aragón". Sos del Rey Católico. (Saragossa).

△ 288 Parador "El Emperador". Fuenterrabía. (Guipúzcoa).

A TRAVELLER'S NOTES

A TRAVELLER'S NOTES
By Oscar Collazos

By the time we left the frontier post of Bossost behind us, all doubts about the incredible beauty of the Vall d'Aran had been dispelled. If ever I had proposed the adventure of such a journey to my wife, this was surely the occasion for proving whether so many days spent on inquiries, so many hopes placed in a given itinerary, would indeed lead us to the fascination the unknown always holds for the traveller. We had never been extempore travellers; we preferred to have some previous knowledge of our route, gained with the patient prudence one needs to avoid travelling "blind", as it were. And the adventure that was to begin at Viella had been provided for from the moment we first decided to travel round the periphery of this Spain as yet unknown to us, and then to penetrate to its centre and perhaps discover things that the average tourist is either too lazy or too careless to investigate. "You cannot do better than stay at the State-run paradores," we had been told, shortly before we began looking for information in earnest. In fact we knew very little about those old buildings, restored and modernized with the dual intention of preserving a precious architectural heritage and providing bed and board for anyone in need of such things. Besides, we were getting rather tired of the impersonality of hotels, so that this suggestion of travelling from one parador to another, especially when we heard that they were to be found all over Spain, was immediately accepted – despite the pessimism of my wife, at first intrigued about the possible duration of our holiday, which we both wanted to be as long and relaxing as possible.
The first thing that caught our attention was the richness of this area by which we were entering Spain, with its zigzag topography (perhaps at times steeper than the Alps, which we had visited on another occasion) and its numerous traces of earlier ages. Romanesque churches and other buildings of the 12th and 13th centuries began to appear on our route even before we came to Viella, the capital of the valley area, 3195 feet above sea level. Everything we had discovered from guides, maps and other sources had an almost humdrum elementariness about it here, despite the centuries of history that slept in this peaceful, relaxing countryside.
We had arrived early one spring morning and made a rapid tour of the valley, discovering the source of the Garonne, which enters France only a few miles downstream, as though wishing to hide from the curiosity of Spain and only be reborn in all its fullness beyond the frontier. We had been much struck by the simplicity of the houses and the sturdy stone solidity of the churches. Romanesque and Gothic, medieval and modern, these are the constant alternations in the Valle d'Aran. It was only when we arrived at the

Parador outside Viella that we first felt sure that we had really begun our journey, for we needed a rest. My wife decided to have a frugal supper of trout grilled in the Pyrenean style, while I chose something rather more filling: ember-grilled beef with rovellons, *the local red pine mushrooms.*
"Did you know that the word parador *comes from Arabic?" I asked my wife just before going to bed. "They say it may have been in use since the year 711 and the original Arabic form is* waradah*."*

△ 1

THE VALL D'ARAN PARADOR IN VIELLA

In the most spectacular scenery the Pyrenees can offer us, the Parador of Viella welcomes us to the fabulous Vall d'Aran barely five kilometres after driving through the tunnel of Viella.
It has all the air of a great mountaintop hotel in its unparalleled location amidst an exhibition of lofty and low-lying views of different panoramas, speckled here and there by plastic mini-villages which pop up on emerald-green meadows, or discreetly take cover behind golden, dark, overwhelming or faded forests, depending on the season in which we catch them unawares.
At other times they are like fanciful dreams enshrouded by the mist which descends from the high summits – Mounts Aneto and Maladeta deserve special mention, standing 3,404 and 3,313 metres respectively – which are covered year-round by a hood of snow.
And at our feet is the poetic contrast of the Garonna; this river which is born in the Vall d'Aran and spends its full bloom of childhood here before adopting French nationality. The Garonna and its tributaries, the Barradós, Nere, Negre, Inyola, Aigüenoix, Jueu and Salient, are mostly trout rivers and paradises for fishermen who can find a whole range of exquisite trout there, not to forget the indescribable "cabilet", which are scrumptious morsels favoured by the natives and caught in the rivers as well as mountain lakes.
But now we are going to check in at the Parador and, after taking an eyeful of all the surroundings, we shall have to face up to the problem of selecting which routes to take of the many – to cover all of them would require an unlimited stay – unbeatable and equally attractive ones available.
Viella, hub and capital of the valley, is two kilometres away. From it there is a whole circuit of villages just a stone's throw away. Each one of them has sufficient artistic and picturesque merits as well as the charm of their characteristic streets, old houses with wooden balconies, and mostly Romanesque churches with sharply-pointed belfries which are very typical of the valley; all of this is covered by a subtle and mysterious aura which emanates from all of the Vall d'Aran, "the most autonomous after Andorra".
I think it is best that we start our itinerary in Viella, as our most nearby excursions will start from there.

Viella is of special interest to us because of its cosmopolitan air, its banks, pleasant hotels, restaurants, roads, shops, and boutique which are all a real temptation for any visitor.
And, amidst this modern, brilliant and international atmosphere, is the elegant impression of its dignified 18th-century houses, its characteristic church, which is Romanesque in its origins as can be seen in its magnificent façade with a stone Christ carved under the intrados. It was remodelled in the 16th century through the addition of a large octagonal bell-tower, and topped off by a long pointed spire which has its counterpoint in the smaller hexagonal side tower.
Amongst the valuable treasures inside are two excellent altarpieces, one from the 15th century and the other 18th-century Baroque; a very interesting Romanesque baptismal font; the marvellous head and torso of the Mig-Aran crucifix, which is a fragment remaining from a large incomplete 16th-century descent from the Cross considered "the greatest and most dramatic of the Romanesque Crucifixes in the Pyrenees". It is a truly remarkable carving, with a beautiful expression masterfully caught by the work of the sculptor of the famous Salardú crucifix.
Finishing this visit a surprise awaits us in the village: the Nere and Sallent rivers, arteries of Viella, which rush headlong cascading between the streets.
From Viella we can take a two-kilometre walk on foot to one of these tiny and picturesque villages which we come across here, there and everywhere: Casau. It forms a pretty skyline and lyrical illuminated backdrop at twilight and on moonlit nights when its lights reveal it for us on the heights.
Closer still is Gausach and its very modern sports complex. The church is its advance guard and has a hexagonal tower, an interesting crucifix between the arches of its main doorway as well as an uncommon Roman tombstone.
Returning to Viella, which is, as we know, at the centre of the lowest part of the valley, we have two routes to follow, both of incomparable beauty.
We shall start with the western one, on which two villages deserve a special visit. Reaching them is a peaceful short stroll and in less than two kilometres we reach tiny, casual Betrén on the roadside.
Only the simple and solid tower remains of the old church. However, it does have a very charming small

church in which Romanesque and Gothic are joined together in its two façades. On one of them there is an attractive rose window and a large window with a column in the centre. On the Romanesque one there is a nice doorway with finely decorated capitals and a triptych of the Virgin and the Holy Infant escorted by angels. This whole church is a filigreed delight: its apses, its windows and the carved figures of two warriors adorning an ornate window.
At one kilometre from this village we come to Escunyau, in which there are some stately houses with Gothic coats-of-arms on their walls, and outside the village, next to the small cemetery, is the church which preserves intact a 12th-century doorway with very noteworthy ornamentation. The Romanesque baptismal font has some very fine high-relief carvings, as does the holy water font. It is worth taking note that almost all of the churches in the valley possess the best baptismal fonts in the Pyrenees, which are carved out of one rock and are sometimes used for baptisms by immersion.
And now we shall return to Viella because the remaining villages are closer to a different Parador.
As I mentioned before, Viella will be the starting-point of our outings. Now we shall head towards the east where some fascinating villages await us. Vilach is the most flourishing and has a 13th-century church which has been so rebuilt that it is almost entirely a copy of what time and the normal course of events had worn down. Before the church there is an enormous parvis covered with rosebushes and other plants which, in these places with pure fresh air, envelop us in a fragrance unknown to big-city dwellers. Vilach is located in a site of great scenic beauty. To reach it we must ascend a road bordered with cliffs at the bottom of which the Garonne river seems to be enjoying itself with cascades and falls. From this road we can enjoy some splendid views of Viella, Gausach and the mountains, as well as the banks of the Nere river.
The village itself is also very beautiful and colourful, with its sloping streets flanked by 17th-century houses with coffered balconies.
Straight afterwards is Mont and very near to it is Montcorbau, with a strong mediaeval flavour and an attractive church looming up over the poetic Garonna. One of the very interesting baptismal fonts which I mentioned earlier is here.
It is worthwhile carrying on to Aubert, a picturesque and primitive village without comparison. It has a charming 12th-century church with a very fine tower on which some extremely unusual figures of saints can be seen. Entrance to the church is gained by an outside staircase; although the portal is rather modest it is amply made up for by the "Crismón" (a monogrammatic device of Christ) and the Romanesque figures adorning it. And we can still go on to see other villages, other churches and other views; we could cross the mountains of Barradós with the river Barradós flowing by at the bottom of a deep gorge and forcing its way through the ferns. On the left is the Mall de l'Artiga Peak and, further on, the Aneto.
There are so many mountain hikes to start from Viella that we cannot make up our minds. So we start with Les Bordes, a collection of shepherds' cabins scattered over the mountainside and forming a municipality centring on a rustic and primitive church and along the Jueu river basin as far as the Pla de la Artiga, surrounded by beech groves and giant pines, near the imposing Jueu waterfall from the top of which the impressive Pumero peak can be seen. Some wonderful excursions can be made from here by going along to Artiga de Lin near the Jueu river, and then to the Güells ("eyes" in the native tongue of the Vall d'Aran), which is an unusual geological phenomenon, and finally reaching the welcoming hiker's mountain refuge.
The splendid Barìcauba woods can be reached from Viella via Gausach, after which we can reach Les Bordes. Following the Garonna to Barradós, we can climb the Pla de la Artiga between some awesome woods in which roe deer, wild boars, foxes, mountain lions, genets and, occasionally, otters live. The capercaillie, almost a symbol of the valley, partridge, quail and blackbirds all nest in the Baricauba woods.
There are also numberless very beautiful lakes with legends, outstanding flora and shores all surrounded by the sounds of nature. They are all quite easy to reach from Viella, especially the lakes of the woods in the Malditos mountains.
It goes without saying that the cooking in the Vall d'Aran is excellent, with nature providing the basic ingredients. Game and fish are easy to find and any restaurant will prepare them expertly.
If the weather is cold, we should not forget to savour a glass of "vincau" after our little stroll or long hike. It will return all the energy we have spent, and as its name in the language of the Vall d'Aran – a mixture of Gascon, Catalan and French according to the philologists – indicates, it is a hot wine punch which is very similar to the Bavarian glühwein preferred by the Alpine shepherds.
I once wrote that the Vall d'Aran was one of the last paradises in Europe and the valley clearly backs me up. I have no doubt that after having stayed at the Parador of Viella the visitor will agree with me.

Carmen Nonell

We got up early next morning and, though our next destination was to be the Seu d'Urgell, we decided to make a detour first to Arties, on the way to Bielsa and Ordesa. So we left the Vall d'Aran and made our way to another corner of the Pyrenees. In fact the Huesca Pyrenees are very similar to the mountains around Viella, though at first sight they may seem even steeper. One is constantly astonished afresh by the spectacle of these heights, which reach a peak of practically eleven thousand feet in that compact mass of rock known as Monte Perdido ("Lost Mountain"). But even on this spring morning the cold is soon dissipated by the intense noonday sun. The 112 miles from Viella to the "Monte Perdido" Parador may seem rather too long a distance, but my wife at once agrees that we should make this journey before spending the night at the Seu d'Urgell. While Arties is only a stop on the way, though none the less attractive for that, for practical reasons our excursion today includes Bielsa. The intensity of the light, at times kaleidoscopic, is really dazzling; there is something miraculous about the sight of these towering, still snowclad mountains. In the Valle de la Pineta we admire the peculiarly Aragonese character of the area, though we still find, as in the Vall d'Aran, Romanesque and Gothic side by side.

Attracted by curiosity and hunger alike, we stopped at Javierre, where we visited the church of Santa Eulàlia de Mérida, a real jewel of the 12th century. Then we had lunch at an inn just a mile or so from Bielsa, where we ate cordero al chilindrón *(lamb garnished with tomatoes and peppers) for the first time in our lives.*

On a stroll through Bielsa we were struck by the balance displayed by this little 16th-century town, just about 10 miles from our next destination, the "Monte Perdido" Parador. In the background, the mountains that form the Franco-Spanish frontier. If only we had time, we could drive through the Bielsa-Aragnonet tunnel. Unfortunately, even these brief 17 miles joining the two countries would take us too long. We must console ourselves with another, equally breathtaking, vision: the river Cinca in the background and, standing out above it, the sober building of the Parador. Behind it, mountains in an almost perpetual mantle of snow. The very seclusion of the place (and I imagine that a few weeks from now the light will be even more intense) is probably just as relaxing – though only for about thirty people, which is its maximum capacity – as the gently undulating landscape. I will always remember this valley of migratory herding, with its typical Pyrenean houses, big or small, huddling together as though the better to protect themselves from the intensity of the cold. No sign of arrogance about them, for the only arrogance one experiences here is that of nature. Everything else (buildings, villages, people) seems to be characterized by a sort of humility that comes from their being caught, as it were, between the unpolished rusticity of their past and the rare intrusions of contemporary civilization.

△ 6

THE "MONTE PERDIDO" PARADOR Bielsa (Huesca)
"LOST MOUNTAIN"

There are names that are so explicit that they make any description unnecessary. On the other hand, there are others that almost manage to distract your attention from their true nature. The Monte Perdido curiously takes in both characteristics. Situated in the middle of the Pyrenees of Huesca, facing France, within a mountainous mass of wild beauty, the Monte Perdido, at an altitude of 3,352 mts., suggests an undiscovered and almost inaccessible spot. And yet there is something about it, in fact. Something, but not everything. For example, from Bielsa, 15 kms. away, you can easily reach the Parador situated at the foot of the mountain at the not inconsiderable height of 1,320 mts., or from

France, going through the Aragnonet tunnel that passes through the mountain for about 2000 metres. You can get there easily, but not indifferently. The valley of La Pineta is rather more than picturesque scenery. Its vegetation and brilliance of colour harmonise so that even the most hardened of travellers cannot do other than surrender himself before such an explosion of beauty. Nature, at the same time gentle and rugged, still holds these surprises. The smoothness of the Valley of the Ribera de la Pineta, contrasts with the watchful presence, not so far away, of the permanently snow-capped summits, or almost, of the glaciers of the rocky peaks that do not cut off the horizon but prolong it vertically towards the clean blueness of a sky that can only be found in the Pyrenees. Anybody can check that it is not a question of a trite cliché but, purely and simply, a self-evident fact.

In fact, there is nothing more diverse and varied than the mountain. Not even the sea can compete with this constant unfolding of changes these mountain landscapes offer, not only with the passing of the seasons (which in these areas accentuate their peculiarities and contrasts), but even in the passing of a day itself. Lights, colours, sparkles, hues, skylines are transformed into a tireless catherine wheel that resembles a kaleidoscope, in order to offer the spectator a limitless variety of countryside. A countryside that in these places decks itself out with an incredible variety of plants which, with the special light and sunshine of these altitudes, find their colouring altered in the passing of a day. This phenomenon, as Henry Myhill recalled, is not an optical illusion but the result of the action of ultraviolet rays. The mountain, then, in the Monte Perdido is something more than an attraction or a photographic setting: it is the possibility of communing with nature in its purest state, still unblemished by that immense despoiling capacity in man. The solitude of the peaks, the tenuous mystery of the woods, the pleasing undulation of the meadowland of Alarri, the springs that further on will turn into rivers (the Cinca starts a little more than 100 mts. from the Parador) make up a picture difficult to equal and difficult to forget for the traveller who can and should make this his stopping and resting place.

Because, what is more, the walks and excursions can easily lead to objectives not necessarily complementary. For instance, only a stone's throw from the Parador is a lovely example of Romanesque architecture, Aragonese style: the hermitage of La Pineta, one of those rural Romanesque examples of these lands that fits in perfectly with the countryside. As is also, and this is now a major example, the little church of Javierre, 2 kms. from Bielsa, built in the 12th century with a notable Gothic altarpiece of the 15th century and a frontal (decorative hanging for the front of the altar) painted at the beginning of the 14th century. A good artistic complement for the lovers of the purity of these parts. And since we are talking of Romanesque, it is a must for any visitor to go to Ainsa, where the rivers Ara and Cinca come together, off the beaten track and, unfortunately, also beyond the appreciation of those responsible for the conservation of the historic and artistic heritage of Spain. Ainsa, capital of the old kingdom of Sobrarbe which joined the kingdom of Aragon in the 11th century, in spite of its isolation, was a constant scene of battles between Christians and Moors. From this it derives its fortress-like character. It still has an exceptional main square with a portico of large and harmonised proportions and a Romanesque church in which a magnificent tower 30 mts. high and a curious façade built from parts of other buildings stand out. In Ainsa, the medieval is something more than a relic: it is the living proof of a past that refuses to perish despite centuries-old neglect and abandon. Without any reservations, a visit is well worth-while. And still on this route, and for more hardened travellers who are not put off by a few discomforts but who take delight in discovering things, close to Ainsa yet difficult to reach with a conventional vehicle, lies Santa Maria de Buil, a small township of Sobrarbe which retains, in a manner of speaking, or rather barely maintains erect, two Romanesque churches, Santa Maria and San Martin. The discomfort of the journey will be amply compensated by the sight of the Sierra de Brell and, once inside the village, by the church of San Martin, before its foreseeable, and seemingly inevitable, collapse ruins this singular example in the varied collection of Romanesque architecture of Aragon.

But let us return to the Parador. The examples that we have mentioned of the Romanesque ruins of Aragon, scattered through these parts, are not the only ones — far from it. None of them are masterpieces of an art which has, in this same province, outstanding and spectacular examples such as the cathedral of Jaca, San Juan de la Peña, Santa Cruz de Serós, among others, which justly fill the pages of the history of art. But, in their humility, they constitute a magnificent and unforgettable complement for those who want to spend their time touring these beautiful lands in the Pyrenees. Nature and art are something more than a complement. In reality, they form an indivisible unity for one who wants to rise above the monotony of the daily routine. There is nothing better for a trip or a stay than synchronising and harmonising the meeting with the beauty of nature and the search for artistic treasures, no matter how simple they are, which history has strewn over these Aragonese lands. In reality, every traveller knows that the triangle of any pleasure trip has its vertices in the scenery, the art and the gastronomy. And of the three, the Parador of Monte Perdido can offer something more than a modest collection of samples. To it one would have to add other atractions, fundamental for many people, such as fishing and hunting. Let us not forget that the Cinca is a river where trout abound and that the ibex (wild mountain goat) called "sarrio" in this region, shows its independent nature, roaming freely throughout the area.

Who has not dreamed sometime of feeling isolated by the snow or wandering for hours in the forest? Who has not been tempted by the call of the mountain tops? Who does not aspire to be transported there where the air is still uncontaminated by dust and the scenery has not suffered the erosion and manipulation of man? The Monte Perdido awaits you. With its winter snows or its joyful springs. And with those summers that require a night blanket and a comforting snack beside a sparkling and welcoming fire. To say that all the hustle and bustle has been left behind is abundantly obvious. But it is not so to say that nowhere so well as in these spots can the true dimension of time and its inestimable value be discovered. Time for walking, for reading, for sport. Time, in short, for oneself. To look within by looking around you. To still enjoy what remains of nature and discover, whether in passing or in planned harmony, it does not matter, that there still exist places where you can contemplate through absolutely clear waters the fleeting glimmer of the fish, the majestic forays of the goats and the unrivalled harmony of the Romanesque apses. And all of it set in that profound freedom that extends through the mountain peaks. Lose yourself – it is not a worn-out phrase – in the Monte Perdido. It is advice from a friend and an incitement, if not to adventure, then to those discoveries that, when all is said and done, reconcile mankind to Mother Nature.

Pedro Altares

The Seu d'Urgell, which is the capital of the Alt Urgell, is full of echoes from its eventful history. A bishopric since the year 527 and practically on the border of Andorra, through which one can get to France, it is also the frontier of a Catalonia so ancient as to be lost in the geography of different peoples. Acting on the suggestion made by some people in Bielsa, we decided to make the gentle descent to the valley of Benasque and then drive across that part of the country as far as the Aragon-Lleida frontier before taking the road to the Seu. An apparently purposeless detour, but amply compensated by the discovery of the rough scenery of Aragon: high, craggy mountains, with narrow, twisting roads. Though this made for a rather tiring drive, the lovely May evening helped to relax us. And so to another frontier: France and Andorra, the great Republic and the tiny Principality. We had penetrated the Pyrenees and now to them we returned. To our surprise we discovered that the Seu d'Urgell even has an airport, communicating it with Barcelona and thence with all the other cities in Europe. The history of this town is long indeed; its Cathedral, which is almost eleven centuries old, is the mute witness to another history: that of the Catalan language. For the chroniclers recall that it was here, in the 13th century, that the first documents written in that language were found. This might seem an unimportant detail, but on our journey we had already discovered for ourselves the sturdy permanence of this tongue in all the nuanced variety of its dialects and even in its intrusions into other languages, like the delightful patois they speak in the Aragonese Pyrenees.

We arrived at the Seu at nightfall. It had been a hard day and our minds would need time to put impressions and images in order. So we decided to explore the town the next morning, but before dinner we had already visited the Cathedral, which is very near the Parador. My wife had been so hard at work consulting guides and manuals that we had hardly unpacked our bags in our sober but very comfortable room when she said:

"Let's go down to dinner at once; I'm hungrier than Hannibal and all his hosts."

"Well," I answered, "no Carthaginian, or even Roman, could be hungrier than I am myself," which had the effect of recalling to her mind the constant presence of warring Muslims in this area.

"I would suggest some cold meats first," said the maître, "and then some nice rabbit with allioli.*"*

This was the first time we had tasted this strong sauce made of garlic and oil (first cousin

to the Provençal aïoli*). But we were to have it again on several occasions in different parts of Catalonia.*
Before going up to our room again, I asked at the reception desk for some information about the district.
"You mustn't fail to visit Ponts, quite near here, and above all its Castle of Sant Pere*. And you should stop at Coll de Nargó, which is on your way there, where you will see the church of Sant Climent and its beautiful bell-tower. There is none like it in all Catalonia."*
Huge walls and ramparts, ancient gateways, fortresses. The Middle Ages live again in this architecture. My wife would have liked to know more about the influence of the Dominicans in this part of the country. But I, perhaps less orthodoxly Christian, was led to think of the Cathars and their extermination in the open warfare that existed between the official Church and the heresies of the time.
The road from the Seu d'Urgell to Vic passes through Puigcerdà, capital of the Cerdanya region. At an altitude of almost 4000 feet, Puigcerdà has the characteristics of a fairly important town, in which the traces of its erstwhile splendour can be seen in old buildings and in the local pride of the townsfolk. From the Carrer de Florensa one can see the Cerdanya stretching away in the distance, clean and open. France is not far off, for a considerable part of the Cerdanya is actually in the neighbouring country. Even if it was so short, the visit to Puigcerdà was very pleasant. But now we had to start going down again, on our way to Vic. Dizzily twisting mountain roads and villages that come to life not only in the winter sports season but also in summer, when they are the favourite resorts of many people from Barcelona, Lleida and Girona. Between Puigcerdà and the steep little town of Ripoll, still high up in the mountains, we tried to draw up a brief inventory. But it was still impossible; we realized that every mile in our journey was making it harder to put our memories in order. Though we had been in Spain for three days now, we seemed to be still as it were flirting with France, for we were constantly coming up against her frontiers. Now, however, on the road to Vich, we were leaving France completely. Ripoll, which is the capital of the surrounding Ripollès district and is only 2270 feet above sea level, begins to give us the feeling that we are descending, not exactly to the sea, indeed, but to the Osona region, which is practically next door to Barcelona. And on our way down we would come to our next goal.
Vic, with an altitude of 1588 feet, was also a great centre of Catalan Romanesque art and has been a bishopric since the year 616. We had never seen before, in such a comparatively small area, such a wealth of art and architecture, so much of a glorious past, the whole summed up in the figure of a founder: the rather unfortunately named Guifré el Pelós ("Wilfred the Hairy"). The town was first Romanesque and then Gothic, awakening to the modern age in the 18th century. But Vic is above all its church, where all its periods meet, past and present mingling in a strange ritual. Vic and the surrounding villages (Folgueroles, Vilanova de Sau, Tavèrnoles, Roda de Ter, etc.) gave us fresh heart for the journey as we approached the sea, which we had not yet seen. So we preferred to imagine that sea for the moment.
"Vic or Cardona?" asked my wife, by now familiar with our itinerary. A difficult choice. I think of the old castle of Cardona, now the "Duques de Cardona" Parador, only 56 miles from Barcelona and very close – too close, indeed – to Vic. And I remember all I have heard about that castle, which goes back to the 10th century, with its church of Sant Vicenç and the mausoleum of Count Joan Ramon Folch; and, above all, the legend:

"They say that in the 15th-century tower called the Maiden's Tower a daughter of the Viscount of Cardona was imprisoned because she had fallen in love with a Moor, who for his part had abjured his faith, possibly to make himself more acceptable to his mistress. The maiden died in the solitude of her imprisonment, as much from a broken heart as from the hard stone walls that surrounded her."

We finally decided on Vic, however, though still hoping to make a brief journey to Cardona the next morning.

We had already read something about the magnificence of the Diocesan Museum in Vic. But sometimes what you read falls short of what you find in reality, and this was our impression when we had made our way through this museum. Once again the centuries seemed to come together. We had been told that in Vic the past ages live in the memory of the townsfolk, and nothing could be truer. All towns in time acquire their patents of gentility, their historic stature. It is their sons, of all periods, who renew their past by dint of remembering it. The narrow, twisting streets bear the stamp of other days. Even though they may deteriorate at the hands of men, who sometimes wish to know nothing of the past and are equally ignorant of what they want for the future, these old towns cannot hide what they once were. It pleased us to arrive at the Parador by a road that seemed to lead only to its surroundings, as though from those surroundings we entered its interior directly. We had barely arrived in our room when my wife opened the window to have a look at the scenery. It took our breath away; we stood there silently – not in meditation or distantly, but in silence. Gone was the overwhelming scenery of the Pyrenees, the steep walls of mountains always on one side as we drove down along river valleys through the Aragonese province of Huesca. Here before us lay a vast, broad valley, with no sign of mountains, a promise of the sea we were soon to reach.

To get to Aiguablava there is no need to go through Barcelona. And so the capital of Catalonia, and second city of Spain, could be left for the next itinerary. We left Vic (not without regrets and lingering memories of its excellent sausages and grilled bread and tomato, or its fabulous market) and drove down to the motorway that takes you to the province of Girona. One may reach the Costa Brava without difficulty, preferably by one of the exits for Palamós or Palafrugell. Wherever you go hereabouts (and this same motorway takes you to the French frontier at La Jonquera), the road will lead to the Costa Brava. Or to the Mediterranean. Or to that song by Joan Manuel Serrat that talks of "a hundred ports from Algeciras to Stamboul". To the Mediterranean, in short. In La Bisbal the south came upon us and my wife, at first reluctant to try some of the more eccentric dishes of the region, was finally persuaded to taste what seemed an extremely heterodox dish. In Catalonia it is called de mar i terra *("of sea and land") and is simply an exquisitely subtle combination of fish or shellfish and "land meats": that is to say veal or lamb, pork or chicken, cooked with prawns, langoustines or even lobster. And it suddenly reminded me of Josep Pla's* El quadern gris *(The grey notebook), a book charged with resonances of the Mediterranean. In this book, years before, I had discovered the measured sensuality that characterizes the people of the Empordà, this northeastern coastal strip of Catalonia. Coming back to the region now, I saw how extraordinarily lucid the writer's view had been. This was the first time on this trip that we let ourselves be wooed into the spontaneous, not only by the insistence of the owner of the inn where we were eating but also by the example of neighbouring tables, where nobody displayed any squeamish scruples about loading the board with food or ordering up yet more bottles of the local wines. Eventually, however, we went on our way to*

Aiguablava, which lies just north of Palafrugell, a village we passed through after stopping for a while to enjoy the lazy seashore charm of Calella and the more modern attraction of Llafranc.

"Something very odd is happening to me," I said to my wife. "I feel my nerves relaxing, as though all the restrained curiosity of the last few days were being liberated."

We were lucky in the day, a fine, warmly sunny Mediterranean spring day. As we drove deeper into the Baix Empordà, we found ourselves remembering – rather vaguely, I must admit – other landscapes, perhaps in the south of France, in Provence. Possibly because the landscape was indeed very similar, with variations so subtle that we did not observe them at first. I noticed this as we drove along the main road to Palafrugell. The very breadth of the Empordà is relaxing (though I have read that the northern part, the Alt Empordà, gradually becomes more sinuous, up there near the French frontier, under the lowering presence of Mount Canigó, that symbol of limits and nationalities). It seems as though the balance imposed by nature were the work of men, of these Catalan pagesos, or peasants, who are hard-working, thrifty and sensual, but are all these things within that sense of measured proportion that is implied in the delightful Catalan word seny.

The Parador at Aiguablava is comparatively new, as is the village around it, once a hamlet of fishermen whose only contact with town life came from an occasional trip to Figueres or Girona, or perhaps a solemn, once-in-a-lifetime visit to Barcelona. Their lives are finely evoked in his books by Pla, that chronicler par excellence of the Empordà. It is in this region, too, that we find something creatively demented: the Tramuntana. I have always been fascinated by the curious resonance of this word that is the name of a persistent Mediterranean wind, like the Mistral, less mysterious.

What a pity to have no time to go further north; from La Escala to Figueres, from Figueres to Cadaqués, from Cadaqués to the Cap de Creus or to Port de la Selva. But we have to stay in Aiguablava. And here there is nothing of antiquity, unless it be the faint traces of the Roman world to be found further inland. The coast, the sea – "the sea, ever and ever beginning again", as I try to recall with Paul Valéry at his most Mediterranean.

Yes, Aiguablava is new; and new, too, was the wine we drank a few hours ago in La Bisbal, though not so new as the very rough red wine we had in Llafranc ("go on, try it, it's our local wine"). Spring light, greenish blue of the sea that reappears later that evening, when we agree to try a suquet de peix – a splendid fish stew which we elect to wash down, to the maître's horror, with a white wine: of a very good brand and as Catalan as the stew, but white. After dinner a stroll, if only to help us digest this local version of the "pot of fish" so frequent all around the Mediterranean. What a pity that we have no time for more than a brief drive around the upper part of the Empordà! We must at least visit Empúries and stop for a few minutes in Sant Martí before returning to the motorway that will take us to Barcelona tomorrow. Aiguablava will probably never know the huge hordes of tourists that flock to the Costa Brava. One gets the idea that the paradores are not designed for crowds, that their very conception, old or new, is aimed at peace and quiet.

△ 23

THE PARADOR OF AIGUABLAVA

The Parador of Aiguablava, in the province of Gerona and the heart of the Costa Brava, is an attractive building that was constructed totally from scratch. Unlike so many other Spanish Paradors, no other ancient and noble edifice was made use of because none existed in these parts. Until the middle of this century Aiguablava had been a place of solitude and paradise set on what we could call the most balanced part of the Costa Brava, well-known for its gaiety, crystal-clear blue sky and calm, yet lively and graceful atmosphere. On this coast there are no large urban centres bordering on the sea, but, on the other hand, there are a great amount of coves or "calas" – a word derived from the Arabic *kalla*, an inlet or sheltered landing – such as the one in Aiguablava. It also has a true richness of tiny beaches with very fine sand, shallow waters and wondrously striking nooks and crannies along the shore. Up to a point we could say that the most illustrative of the Costa Brava is to be found in Aiguablava, Tamariu, Llafranc and Calella de Palafrugell. Any recollection of these places will also be in company with the memory of the vivid and almost palpable light which shines in two unforgettable colours: the most luminous and vibrant blue found in the Mediterranean and the billowy green of the fresh, joyous and exuberant vegetation.
The historical centre of Aiguablava is the town of Begur, of feudal origins, held by the Cruïlles de Peratallada family from the 14th to the 18th century. Their stone castle was destroyed in the 15th century and reconstructed in the 17th; the French later occupied it in the Peninsular War until the Anglo-Hispanic troops recovered it. Begur is situated in a semicircle at the foot of the hill which the castle crowns. It has an unmistakable personality given to it by the defence towers – now national monuments – against pirates and the typical galleries of its houses constructed by the native *Begurenses* who had emigrated to the New World in the 19th century, only to nostalgically, and often much richer, return to their homeland. The roads linking it to Fornells and Aiguablava at four and a half kilometres and to Aiguafreda at about three kilometres make it very strategically located. These are now tourist spots *par excellence* where all water-sports can be enjoyed and from which some extremely interesting trips by sea or land can be started. But, in addition to the summer activities, the sun, the sea and the charm of the countryside, is the age-old hospitality of the villagers. The inhabitants of the lower Ampurdán region are contemplative and negligent, epicurean and jovial, often sceptical and lovers of the little pleasures in life. Both the farmer and the fisherman are fascinating people.
Just as the populace and the countryside are so warm, welcoming and very humane, there is also another outstanding feature for the traveller and visitor: a very precise and authentic cuisine. Gastronomy is a delicate and complex art in which personal inspiration and the local flavour play a particularly important role.
As might be expected, the Costa Brava cuisine is based on fish, although that does not mean that meat dishes do not also reach truly remarkable heights of quality. I still owe my best and most unforgettable experiences as far as cooking fish on the Costa Brava is concerned to that great writer and late friend, Josep Pla, an accomplished expert in so many things. This very noteworthy cuisine has been inspired by the rich variety of fish along the seaboard: dorados, groupers, dentones, like a sea-bream with strong conical teeth, sea bass and red mullet; the three great "blue" fish of our coast: sardines, mackerel and anchovies; as well as all the choice fish which grace the savoury fish soups. These form the basis of this marine cooking which is as old as the olive tree, the sky and the deep blue sea. There are also many delicate and tasty shellfish from which the coastal cooks have concocted some exceptional creations.
The grouper is a rock fish — black and gold, firm and muscular, cruel yet valiant like a salty old pirate. Groupers are used to prepare succulent dishes in all styles: grilled, baked, fried, in a *suquet*, even with rice. Rice with grouper heads is a typical dish in Fornells and can be presented as an example of this varied and flavourful savoir-faire with fish.
Apart from their everyday bills of fare, dentones, sea bass and doradas lend themselves very well to the *suquet*, a common meal on our coast. The *suquet* is really nothing more than a variety of the Mediterranean pot-o'-fish. Depending on the location these fish-stews all have particular traits, reaching sublimity in Provence with the masterly bouillabaisse. The Costa Brava *suquet* can be prepared in a simple old-fashioned way: lightly fry oil, tomatoes, onions, garlic and parsley together, then stew this mixture with potatoes and fish over a blazing bonfire. This plate has a surprising, lively and hard-hitting forcefulness.
The agile and aggressive red mullet is, on our coast, a red mullet with distinction. The red mullet is an outlaw fish, avid and fierce, a glutton for meat. Its quality depends on the life style it leads. Those living on a rocky sea bed with algae are the best: large, round-headed with very firm flesh and turning to a lavish scarlet when cooked. The red mullet is handled with loving care on the coast; it is served braised with garlic and parsley and is sometimes seasoned with a twig of fennel.
Fish soups are always tasty when prepared in a straightforward way. Generally speaking, these soups are always exquisite around the Mediterranean, and on the Costa Brava there is a literally prodigious variety of fish to prepare them with: burras, spider crabs, anglers and, above all, *scorpaena* or gurnards which, on our coast, are the main ingredients for any fish soup which has to be sharp, spicy and aromatic. Any shellfish which come to hand can also be thrown in, and the result can hold its own against any other soup

prepared between Crete and the Spanish village of Cabo de Creus.

In a slightly different hierarchy are the "blue" fish which are of very high quality all along the coast. Sardines prove a mouth-watering breakfast between May and August. Bought when the fishermen return from trawling in the early morning, and braised over pinewood embers while they are still plump and have a glazed and fatty blueness, accompanied by a choice, at times rather acid dry light wine from the vineyards of Ampurias or Llagostera, they can be unforgettable. Mackerel are prepared in the same way but have a stronger taste and need a heavier, fuller-bodied rosé or red wine. The fleshy anchovy is not normally cooked along the coast but rather pickled in brine.

And now we arrive at a dish which, even though it has attained excellent qualities amongst ourselves, can nevertheless lead to immense gastronomic catastrophes. We mean rice, to be more precise, rice with fish. Magnificent fish and rice concoctions based on lightly simmered delicate sauces of onions – mostly – and tomatoes are made on the Costa Brava. Rice with shellfish, a truly extraordinary dish, is prepared with the tiny, bristly and violent spider crab. Rice with conger eels is somewhat milder, but it can reach lofty heights when served with baby peas from the lower Ampurdán. Rice prepared with lobster is more scrumptious and a trifle sweet. Brown rice with its slow, laborious and almost Benedictine sauce of simmered onions is, perhaps, the most exquisite of the entire gamut of rice dishes which have Mediterranean fish as their basis.

The spiny lobster and the lobster proper both contend for the difficult sceptre of sovereignty amongst crustacea. The ever scarcer lobster has an unmistakable hint of something special when braised, especially so when served with a vinaigrette which has been prepared with a gentle Athenian touch. The spiny lobster is also excellent, and there are several marvellous ways of cooking it. The so-called lobster *a la catalana* with a chocolate and biscuit sauce possibly does not stem from this region. What is a characteristic dish is the fabled *langosta y pollo*, or lobster and chicken, eaten in the districts of Palafrugell, Palamós, Sant Feliu and S'Agaró, where it is also known as "sea and mountain" for obvious reasons; this is a majestic and sumptuous dish linked to the secret of an opulent and magical dark-golden sauce which is very hard to get just right. Another dish based on this crustacean is lobster with escargots: the majestic lobster attended by a retinue of dainty snails.

Mussels which grow clinging to wave-swept rocks are excellent, especially if there are filtrations of fresh water reaching them; our coast, however, has become sadly deficient in this regard. They taste most delicious to us when just simply steamed and with the unforgettable hint of their brackish and penetrating odour.

We have yet to mention the traditional complement to many of the dishes on our coast: *allioli*, a garlic and olive oil sauce which originates from Provençal cooking. Josep Pla thought it might have been introduced here at the beginning of the Middle Ages by the monks of the San Pere de Roda Monastery who were stalwarts of fish dishes and jealous defenders of a feudal and authoritative cuisine. The fondness of these Benedictine monks for seasoning fish with garlic is clearly shown in the ancient documents of the thousand-year-old monastery of Sant Feliu de Guíxols. Whatever its origins are, the Mediterranean *allioli* is as time-honoured as fish stew and braised fish.

Nowadays on our coast, aside from these delicacies of the regional cuisine, one can also eat more internationally known dishes, so that all palates are satisfied. Nevertheless, we should like to suggest that the visitor turn his eyes towards the age-old wisdom behind the smells of slowly simmering sauces, robust and somewhat rustic wines, the most commonplace fish, the most elementary rices as well as the spiciest and choicest fish soups – something scarce, quite rare yet magnificently delightful along this Mediterranean seaboard.

The inland cuisine also carries a lot of weight; even though the lower Ampurdán region has a short and delicate growing season, it still produces extraordinarily first-class products. The meats reach truly high levels of quality when they have been raised in the countryside – lambs which graze in seaside meadows, all sorts of pork sausages and, becoming scarcer and scarcer, game. When in season you can still enjoy partridges from Cabo de Creus in Cadaqués and, on the occasions when the winter conditions are right, woodcocks – truly wonderful morsels – can be found in the area of La Selva. But the dominating gastronomical factor in the entire region is pork. All of the sausages are excellent, especially so the "botifarra de perol", a large Catalan sausage with kidney beans, and the "butifarra dulce" from Ampurdán, – a delicacy in which the confectioner and the cook join hands – which are both mouth-watering dishes. In like manner the sweetmeats are excellent, and since there are many Indianos, or Spaniards who emigrated to the New World and returned, coffee plays an important role. The punch-like concoction called *cremat*, espresso coffee with rum, lemon and sugar, drunk in the cheerfully boisterous company of fishermen in a tavern in Llafranc or La Escala, can help you to warmly and fully enjoy life.

Aiguablava and its Parador form the axis of a first-class tourist zone midway along the coast. The illuminated yet filmy mystery of the timeless Mediterranean, rather restrained in its storms, extremely mild in its balmy summers, purply and magical at twilight, shimmering and almost noiseless in the calm summer nights, has the Apollonian gracefulness of the dolphin as its mythological symbol; its silvery leap is the perpetual emblem of the lissomness and becomingness of this Costa Brava which is reborn and renewed at each break of day with its clear, surprising and intact eternally fascinating innocence.

Néstor Luján

We decided to make the return journey a little longer, so as to avoid the motorway which would take us to Barcelona in under two hours. Without the summer crowds, traffic on the old main road is less hectic in the spring. Sant Feliu de Guixols, Tossa de Mar: it is always worthwhile stopping, even though very briefly, at villages on the shores of the Mediterranean. They have grown over centuries and, while they may not usually be historic centres, they do tend to have a very individual stamp. Modern Catalonia is present in these little towns, and as one passes through them one invents a past for them that may well have been less noisy and hurried than their life today. The Costa Brava is modernity itself.

When we finally did get on to the motorway to Barcelona (a city we had visited in earlier years and other circumstances, and one that would need a whole chapter in our travellers' memoirs), we at once felt the full prosperity of Catalonia, as constant in its destiny as it has been disciplined and thrifty in its past. But since we had to press on to Tortosa, we had only fleeting glimpses of the well-tilled Maresme district, the immense vineyards of the Penedès, the Garraf and the Alt Penedès (with its famous monastery of Poblet, traditional last resting-place of the kings of Catalonia and Aragon). We had to deprive ourselves of a visit to the Wine Museum, hurry across the Priorato district which produces such admirably full-bodied red wines, not even enter the historic city of Tarragona, leave Gandesa behind with barely a glance. And finally we came to Tortosa, capital of the Baix Ebre.

"Tortosa was founded in the 3rd century B.C.," my wife remarked, "by Scipio Africanus Major, apparently. And during the Moorish domination it became the capital of one of the petty Muslim Kingdoms. This guide says that the Roman walls of the city were destroyed by the Moors, and that our parador is in the old castle of La Zuda ("The Waterwheel"), which was later renamed Castle of St John."

"The guide should also say something, if I remember rightly, about the statue of Our Lady of the Sash, who is venerated by everybody for miles around."

"And there is also something about the convent of Santa Clara, built in the 13th century."

"Does it say anything about partridges chasseur?"

My wife just smiled, perhaps to reproach me for my growing obsession with the regional specialities.

The medieval Christian and Moorish worlds communing, as in the region of the Terra Alta, with its historic town of Gandesa which we had not had time to visit. And still the limpid light of the "Golden Coast" that we had left at Amposta to come upstream to Tortosa. Fortunately we had arrived after midday and my wife also yielded, after all, to the temptation of the partridges and of an evening stroll round the city after dinner.

△ 26

THE "LA ZUDA" PARADOR

Among the many Paradors I have visited, the one of "Castillo de la Zuda" (La Zuda Castle), situated in Tortosa (90 kilometres from Tarragona), has especially attracted my attention. I spent five days there, resting and exploring the surrounding countryside, the region as a whole, and going on a few trips to very interesting places nearby. Once again I am convinced that the idea of setting up a network of "Paradors" – using, in many cases, historical buildings where the maintenance costs would have been extremely high – was a truly splendid one, so much so that, according to the latest information, it is being copied in various countries in Europe and America.

The Parador, resembling a fortress, is 59 metres above sea level and covers about 435,000 square metres. The name "La Zuda" probably comes from the well that, according to Arab authors, was built in the enclosure in the time of Abderramán II, around the year 944, a well

which still exists today in the grounds of the Parador. The hill where the Parador is situated forms a rocky mass that dominates the monumental city of Tortosa. The primitive walled structures date from the Romans, who built them on the ruins of a very early Iberian village. Its initial purpose was to serve as a look-out over the low valley of the Ebro. In the Middle Ages the Castle was converted into the royal residence and the seat of the law courts. The underground dungeons, still existing today, served as jails. King Jaime I chose it as his favourite residence and from there planned the reconquest of Morella, capital of the Maestrazgo, Peñíscola and Burriana. The present Parador still has various vestiges of successive reconquests.
In the entrance to the Parador, after having climbed the steep hill making it accessible from the plain, one can read, on a type of mural altarpiece, an inscription by the poet Al-Gaziri which says:

> At the summit of a stark height,
> Where no one could hope to find comfortable refuge,
> The ravens squawk and perch on the summit,
> And on it you can hear the winds blowing.
> Those who have climbed it once in their life
> Often complain of having felt their hearts weaken.

Without a doubt, these lines constitute a negative challenge for the traveller; however, it is evident that they were written when the aforementioned climb of the hill would have been very difficult. Nowadays, the asphalted road with no obstacles permits one to climb it, even on foot, without any difficulty. For example, only a few minutes are needed to climb from the Cathedral situated at the foot of the hill, which is one of the most beautiful Catalan Gothic Cathedrals.
The four-star "La Zuda" Parador, inaugurated in 1976, after a lot of hard work, as the fortress was in ruins, has seventy-two double rooms and nine singles available, a total of 153 beds. All the rooms have bathrooms and terraces and their most distinguishing feature, as in the whole building, is their cleanliness. On the walls there are paintings and antique engravings. In any corner one can find sculptures or genuine ceramics. It naturally has all the necessary services: restaurant, bar, children's park, swimming pool, central heating, television room, etc. I stayed there in winter and I can assure the reader that the atmosphere was very friendly, in spite of the fact that outside there were hurricane winds reaching a velocity of 120 km. per hour. A bit of an anomalous circumstance given that the climate of the region, the littoral of Tarragona, is usually one of the most pleasant in our geography. Aside from the walls, the dining room and conference room deserve a special mention. In the conference room conventions, assemblies and seminars are held. It was not easy to adapt the ancient walls and the solid doorways to a modern functional use; however, an equilibrium has been achieved. Thanks to the woodwork, the carpets, the wrought iron, the beautiful glasswork, etc., the very diverse styles have been bound together into an admirable unity.
"La Zuda" Castle is situated in the inner part of the city of Tortosa. Its turret, called the Point of the Diamond, seems to be the origin of the fortress and the nucleus around which was built the city, in which according to the census of 1970 there were 46,376 inhabitants. Recently various municipalities have been separated from it, causing a decrease in population. Despite that, it continues to be, aside from being the Episcopal Seat, one of the biggest townships of Catalonia, bordering on Valencia and the lower part of Aragon, whose influences have been great, including the idiosyncrasy of its inhabitants. Many famous people have come from Tortosa; among those who should be mentioned are the Carlist General Cabrera, the brilliant painter Francisco Gimeno and the politician Marcelino Domingo. Those who have been closely linked to the city are the musician Juan Lamote de Grignon, founder of the Liceo in Barcelona, the famous antipope Benedict XIII *(Papa Luna)*, who lived there for certain periods of time and of whom, in the Museum, various exceptional mementos still exist.
The region is rich, thanks to the Ebro, its vertebral artery. Its economy is traditionally based on agriculture, with intensive crops of olives, carob trees, rice, orange groves, etc. Various foreign companies have recently invested vast sums of money in an attempt to improve production in the land of the Ebro Delta, a must for the traveller in these parts and within easy reach of any guest at the Parador.
The Delta greatly impressed me, even though I visited it during a time of great drought. Measuring 20 kilometres long, it constitutes one of the most significant geographical phenomena of Catalonia. Possessing a network of irrigation ditches and canals dating from time immemorial, the Ebro, which one crosses by ferry, is divided into two areas that flow into it on both sides of the island of Buda, which form in the south the Port of the Alfaques and in the north El Fangar. In both areas one can see not only the type of beaches and 'barracas' (thatched farmhouses) described by Blasco Ibáñez and Juan Sebastián Arbó, but also mirages as remarkable as the ones in the Sahara. The traveller becomes lost in the labyrinth of roads that interweave everywhere, losing sight of them, surrounded by ricefields and a fauna in which they have counted no fewer than 36 species of fish, 27 of mammals, 12 of reptiles and 237 of aquatic birds. Fishing enthusiasts will find something there which will more than satisfy their interest in maritime and freshwater fishing. Ecologists complain, justifiably so, of the modern use of pesticides, but nature is defending itself as best it can.
For the hunting enthusiast, "La Zuda" Parador is also strategically situated. In record time one can reach the mountain pass of Beceite-Tortosa, dominated by the Monte Caro, 1,447 metres high, where, under the control of the ICONA, one can find one of the biggest

and most sought-after hunting reserves in Spain. In the aforesaid mountain range of Tortosa, in addition to mountaineering, one can come across the most beautiful examples of "capra hispánica" (ibex), whose numbers are estimated at about 7,000. The presence of cynegetic teams coming from distant lands provides, once the season draws near, one of the attractions of the Parador.

At only 3 kms. from "La Zuda" one can also find the Ebro Observatory, whose importance has been unanimously recognised. At the moment, it is the "World Centre of Rapid Magnetic Variations" (more than 80 observatories on our planet monthly send their data there).

A Parador, in short, open to any whim of the most demanding traveller. The meals can be either international or regional, depending on taste. The fish caught in the Delta are the basis for a long list of original dishes, like eel, young eels and frogs' legs. In pastrymaking, there still exist specialities of the court of the aforementioned *Papa Luna*, such as "garrofetes del Papa". The so-called "Pastissets de Tortosa" are left over from the Arab confectionery. As to the rest, a few deserve a separate mention, like the sherbets, ice cream and, above all, perfectly cooked "crema catalana" (a type of cold custard).

I have very pleasant memories of my stay in "La Zuda". It is not necessary to go out of one's area to spend a very enjoyable holiday, in a peaceful atmosphere, to which history and archaeology contribute a fair amount and dominate the Parador. Whoever wishes to broaden his horizons has at hand, I repeat, a series of day trips which must include a visit to Tarragona, where the Romans left imperishable traces. The patron saint of Tortosa is the Virgin of the Sacred Sash (Santa Cinta), whose relic disappeared in 1936 during the Spanish Civil War and was found much later, precisely in my home town of Darnius (Gerona). It was a surprising fact that evoked in me an emotive imprint that the spirit always wishes to find when one sets off to discover unknown lands and places.

José María Gironella

Now we must return to Gandesa and take the road to Alcañiz. We shall not meet the members of the Order of Calatrava, who once had their chief seat there, but one thing we will find is a very material sign of the generosity of Alfonso II: the imposing monastery-castle "of Concord", now the Parador. Just 62 miles from Tortosa, Alcañiz has a Baroque cathedral with a façade, as they will tell you, that is second only to that of Murcia. We are surrounded here by the history of the Maestrazgo region, with all the vicissitudes of its mountain warfare. We will have time to visit some of the nearby towns: Beceite, Calaceite, Valderrobres, Azaila, Molinos, Caspe.

We set out the next morning with all the relaxed curiosity of travellers. The splendid, high-bowered elegance of Calaceite makes us wish we could spend longer in those ascending and descending streets, that fortunately unimpaired equilibrium. Back in Alcañiz, we realize that the spur on which our parador stands, dominates the whole surrounding region. And we rediscover the 15th-century Exchange, now the Municipal Library, and the 18th-century Collegiate Church, so worthily sung by its chronicler, Don Francisco Mariano Nifo, to whose talent as a journalist Alcañiz owes so much.

The previous day's drive through the Maestrazgo has left us for the first time really exhausted. But our night's rest (it is a quiet night in Alcañiz and the chill is nothing like the cold of the Pyrenees) has quite restored us. Again it comes to my mind that what makes the nights so pleasant in these paradores is the peace and quiet, the feeling of wellbeing just before sleep, which is renewed each morning when you open your window and hear only the faintest, most distant of noises.

From Alcañiz we have driven to Morella and from there down to Vinaroz. Then a short stretch of the main road takes us to Benicarló, on the "Orange-blossom Coast", and almost beside it the lively seaside resort of Peñíscola. Some traces of 16th-century Baroque reveal the comparative antiquity of the town, which in late May, with the tourist season just about to begin, is already livening up. My wife is impatient to try the local fish and rice dishes, and she decides we must have lunch at one of the local restaurants. Once installed in the discreetly modern "Costa del Azahar" Parador, for the first time on this trip we yield to the temptation to "step back into the world" for a moment, as my wife puts it. In fact the papers have no extraordinary news, but the very relaxation we get from looking through them as we sip our sangría in the bar brings us back to the feeling of being in transit, so to speak, of having momentarily stopped the course of events – a feeling often experienced by travellers, whose sole concern sometimes seems to be their arrival at the next stage on their route. After lunch we visit Peñíscola, only about four miles away. Then we go on along the coast to Benicasim (37 miles) and branch off a little further south to take the road to Teruel. We have forgotten what day it is. Dates no longer seem to matter.

△ 28

THE "COSTA DE AZAHAR" PARADOR IN BENICARLÓ

Other paradores in Spain were established in the noble shells of what were once castles, mansions or Renaissance manufactories. The ghosts of other centuries are in their very foundations and the traveller can sleep, perhaps uneasily, in the erstwhile royal suite, breakfast in his lordship's stables fitted out as a dining room, or stroll through tapestry-hung granite halls under extinct coats of arms. The 'Costa de Azahar' Parador may not be housed within such venerable walls, but it does possess a treasured political and literary remembrance, for it was here that Manuel Azaña set that late stage dialogue entitled "Evening in Benicarló".

The plan for a network of paradores only really got under way during the Second Republic, and the then Hostel of Benicarló was built in 1933, with the white simplicity of an elegant monasticism and a rather hygienic air about it that appealed only to English lay visitors – who were, in any case, the only tourists who really appreciated our country in those days. In 1966 the building was enlarged, with modern wings designed to appeal to the taste of Mr Hilton and his patrons, and all that remains of the sober attractions of its original Republican aesthetic is a few stretches of whitewashed wall and the surrounding countryside. For the true appeal of this Parador, like so many others, is its situation. Benicarló has a Baroque church in its main square and famous prawn beds just off its coast; it is a farming town, with fruit trees, vines, carob trees, vegetables, Moorish waterwheels and ecclesiastical palm trees, and it lies between Peñíscola and Vinaroz in the province of Castellón, just off the Barcelona-Valencia motorway. It makes a good starting-point for exploring the rest of the region.

The Parador faces the sea and four miles of gently curving beach that end towards the south at Peñíscola, where the castle of the antipope Benedict XIII (the "Papa Luna") stands high up on a rocky promontory emerging from the water. Peñíscola, indeed, is a very ancient stronghold, with a history going back to the local exploits of Hamilcar Barca. It meets all the typical tourist's requirements: steep streets, a medieval castle, cool dungeons, old men in black silhouetted against the whitewashed walls.

Gastronomically, Benicarló is the realm of shellfish, lettuce, angler-fish, bogues and sardines; rice comes to it from the Ebro Delta or from Sueca, and it is around here that the orange plantations begin. By this I mean that Benicarló is the real gateway to the ecstatic softness of the south, with that air it has of a big hamlet in a paschal breeze. Here the traveller can find excellent, natural, home-cooked dishes, for the kitchen gardens reach almost into the kitchens themselves; the prawn however, is the true king of the local cuisine.

The country around Benicarló contains both dry and irrigated farmland, and the whole place has an air that is at once maritime and rustic. It belongs officially to the Maestrazgo, though it has none of the wild loneliness of that hilly region, the most typical part of which lies well into the hinterland. The Maestrazgo proper is a region of hills straddling the edges of three provinces: Tarragona, Teruel and Castellón. Yet Benicarló makes a good base for excursions into these jagged mountains with all their medieval remains: San Mateo, which is the capital, Traiguera with its pottery tradition and ruined Roman walls, Catí, which is full of huge 14th-century houses, the walled town of Morella and the mountain passes. It is a land of rather lonely beauty, still virtually unknown and only revealing its secrets to the discerning traveller.

The 'Costa de Azahar' Parador in Benicarló should be made a compulsory stop for the flocks of tourists migrating south. For it is here that the scenery begins to soften; from this very spot one can already sense something of the sweetness of Valencia. Further south we come to the voluptuously curving bay of Oropesa, the charm of Benicasim, still sighing for its bourgeois bathing beauties of the thirties, the city of Castellón and then all the riotous flowering of La Plana, the flat region stretching down to Valencia. Sea, castles, ruins, prawns, good vegetables and emphatically non-glutinous rice. To my mind one cannot – or should not – ask for more.

Manuel Vicent

From the province of Castellón to that of Teruel. We are struck by the appearance of what the local people call the torico, *or "little bull", which, with the solitary star, is the emblem of Teruel. A square here pays homage to the bull, that pre-eminently Hispanic symbol. The wealth of Mudéjar architecture here is as astonishing as the Romanesque of the Cathedral. Tower after tower. This city was consolidated between the 13th and 15th centuries. We meet a man who recommends us to visit "the Arches", which turn out to be the original aqueduct, a fine Renaissance monument if ever there was one. An old town, a truly ancient town.*

"Have you never heard of Isabel de Segura and Diego Garcés de Marcilla?" a young man asks us. From him we learn that Teruel is called "the city of the lovers", because of these two young people and their unhappy fate. We are told, at length, how Diego did his utmost to prevent Isabel's marriage to the wealthy lord of Azagra; how the wedding was clamorously announced by all the bells in the city; and, finally, how the lovers met again and their meeting led to their death – which may have been real or symbolic, but is very really reproduced by the legend. The people of Teruel speak of these lovers as of something of their own, something still living in their communal memory.

"If you want to understand the city at all," another citizen warns us, "you must on no account separate Moors from Christians." The 130-mile journey from Benicarló is like an abyss created by time and two cultures. "Mudéjar Teruel" is another watchword. And to appreciate it we must visit the church of El Salvador, one of the oldest in the city. How can one forget the dramatic beauty of the Christ of the Three Hands enshrined in that church? Or not remember the imposing church of San Pedro, which combines Mudéjar and Romanesque? Was it not in the 15th century that they built the Gothic church of San Francisco, which could not resist the temptation of Mudéjar either?

"Have you seen the menu?" my wife asks. "There is a dessert called 'Nun's Sighs'."

"No, but I've just read that there's another one called 'Angelica of St Camillus'," I reply. Before trying either of these delicacies, however, we both order chicken al chilindrón *(with tomatoes and peppers).*

Albarracín and Bronchales, Mora de Rubielos and Cella: these are some of the names on our route for the folowing day. A note in my diary: "I simply cannot get over it; one would say that all these ages and cultures live together under the same roof." And off we go to Valencia, already in our mind's eye the thin line that divides the great lagoon of the

Albufera from the Mediterranean. Our next stop is at El Saler, 12 miles south of the city of Valencia. It will be pleasant to visit that city again, though we have been there before. In fact we were there for the wild festivities of the Fallas, *with an occasional rest in the shade of the 13th-century cathedral. We did not know Valencia then, and still less during those mad days leading up to the feast of St Joseph (19th March). The sacred and the profane, healthy merriment and excesses, seemed to be the two opposed poles of a single popular instinct. The whole world seemed full of celebrations, fireworks, masks, sensuality, practical jokes. But I will always remember, too, the Merchants' Exchange, evoking the busy trade of medieval Valencia.*

All the way from Valencia to Alicante the road is lined by that most absolutely Mediterranean of all trees, the umbrella pine, with its delicately-balanced silhouette. Soon we will come to El Saler, where we are to spend the night. I am intrigued to discover that the Arabic beni, *or* bini, *means "sons": Benicarló, Benicasim, Benillup. In a passage by an ethnologist I read that many of the Valencian villages were built "in the same form as the Moroccan* dchar*", and that even when they had become part of Christian seigniories, after the expulsion of the Muslims, they maintained their original names. Thus a whole urban organization of Arabic origin lasted much longer than other signs of the same provenance. One must suppose that a long time passed before these villages ceased to be governed through their* alfaquíes, *or religious leaders. A journey into the ancient kingdom of Valencia is like penetrating into worlds which were at odds in politics while perfectly in agreement as to culture. Luxury and ostentation: these are my memories of the fiestas in Valencia. The huge bonfires on St Joseph's Day, with the burning of all the* fallas. *Pageants representing battles between Moors and Christians. They are still kept up here, quite as splendidly as in Alcoy. All this comes to mind, and I think what a pity it is that I have never gone back to Valencia to see the great festivities of St Joseph.*

△ 35

THE LUIS VIVES PARADOR
EL SALER (Valencia)

First of all, there is the sea: the sea with its timeless smile. This silken slice of the Mediterranean with its friendly sands, softly-lulling waves and no solemn myths, offers periods of fascinated contemplation, water sports and beneficial sunshine. The central coast of the Valencian region has hardly any abrupt irregularities; only in nearby Cullera does a bit of mountainous land emerge. And on the other side is the Albufera. The Parador is located in the middle, right on the wide ribbon of dunes and alluvia separating sea and lagoon: an ancient common called La Devesa, now covered with undergrowth and pines, which was a perilous place until a couple of centuries ago. Blasco Ibáñez in *Cañas y Barro* described it as densely wooded, with fearful legends and dangerous beasts, almost a place for prehistoric hunting-parties. It has now been turned into a delightful strip of land trampled over by holiday makers and tourists, somewhat built up – perhaps too much so – yet cheerfully inviting pleasant walks, sports and relaxation.

The countryside in itself is remarkable for its contrasts. The Albufera, a smooth-surfaced marsh which shimmers at any time of day or night, is a veritable geological survival. It has shrunk with time – the victim of natural destruction and the greed of the peasantry. It has been transformed into farmland, mostly rice-fields and orchards, over a large area. Surrounding it are immense plains. Rice, of course, comes first. It is economy as well as gastronomy. The dishes a visitor simply must taste, the "popular cuisine" which must be savoured on its home ground, are prepared with rice. But not only rice. For the most truly typical dish of the Albufera is "allipebre", a spicy eel-stew which is a product of strictly local traditions. However, rice does make itself felt and does so in the form of paella. It may well be that paella was originally suburban fare, linked more closely to the Valencian fondness for huge open-air Sunday dinners than to any indigenous custom. Homemade rice dishes are innumerable; in restaurants an interesting choice is "arròs a banda" – a fishermen's dish with a pleasing and quite out-of-the-ordinary taste.

After the marshes come the "huertas" and "huertos". It does not matter what the Dictionary of the Royal Spanish Academy says, because here *huerta* and *huerto* are different agricultural notions. A *huerta*, or kitchen garden, produces vegetables, while the *huerto* is an orchard, especially of orange trees. And one can at once see the startling differences between them. There is also an occasional vineyard here and there, although they are more abundant further away. A drive through these Valencian districts – insomuch as the countryside is a creation of man's rural efforts – reveals unexpected contrasts. And even more so depending on the calendar.

And then there are museums for all tastes. Not as many as the country could offer, but enough. There are museums of paintings, ceramics, ecclesiastical remains, prehistory and even one of American palaeontology. In Valencia one can admire Goyas, Grecos, Bosches, Velázquezs and the odd Dutch master; some are of doubtful authenticity, but valid on their own account whoever it was who painted them. And there are some glorious illuminated manuscripts in the university library. They are things which the tourist should not ignore. Behind those stones, those canvases, those manuscripts, there is a specific "culture" summed up in illustrious names such as Ausiàs Marc, Joanot Martorell, Luis Vives, the friends of Lope de Vega, Gregorio Mayans.... In Latin, in Provençal, in Catalan, in Castilian and in Italian, a complex literature has come from this small society. The tourist should not leave without at least learning about this – even if only as just another memory.

Next to be accounted for are the fiestas. Valencians in general have always been famous for these. What have become almost clichés are the fallas. Fallas are combustible platforms laden with sarcasm; grotesque figures and pasteboard constructions are made just to be set on fire on the night of St. Joseph. Even more fiery are the pyrotechnics – so penetrating in their noise and showiness. A string of firecrackers or a "mascletada", fireworks of presumably Arab influence, might well be just around the corner. Until 1609 more or less one-third of the inhabitants of Valencia were still Muslim. They were expelled by Philip III. However, they left traces of greater or lesser importance in the vocabulary, certain delicacies and fine arts. Behind the mass-produced glazed tiles of today lurks a subtle and – with time – paled Moorish touch.

Based at the Parador, an alert tourist can discover for himself the complexity and gracefulness of different life styles both past and present, not only thrilling but also conflicting...or he can simply abandon himself to the beach. A longer drive would take us to the much less green and exuberant drylands. The recent and rather timid attempts at industrialization in Valencia have added another tone to our villages: a hasty and improvised modernization which has impaired their ancestral character. But this happens everywhere. Nor have we any right to ask anyone to continue being "typical" just to serve as a showpiece. For example, the *barracas* (Valencian-style farmhouses) have all but disappeared, and quite logically so. Their former inhabitants and their descendants prefer to live in city flats with bathrooms and store-bought sheets.

Over and above the "countryside" comes "history". Not the dry-as-dust history of documents and battles, but rather their residue: monuments. Valencia has many examples of an elegant Gothic in its architecture, with Catalan influence in its most illustrious buildings like the Cathedral, the Llotja (Stock Exchange) and the Torres dels Serrans. And of the Renaissance as well in the Palace of the Generalitat (Seat of the Autonomous Government) and the Corpus Christi Chapel. And there are Neo-Classical buildings and a magnificent example of Rococo in the Palace of the Marqués de Dosaigües – discreet and provincial elegance in the Calle de la Paz. In Sagunto there is the living testimony of Roman images in relief with sumptuous archaeological evidence. There is some late Roman work in Sagunto itself, as well as in Liria, Valencia and Játiva. Játiva and Gandía are the homelands of the Borgias: hallucinating popes, ferocious condottieri, the famous Lucrezia "The Poisoner" and saints like Francis, the Jesuit. There are ruins of castles within a stone's throw. And in passing through Gandía and its environs one can try *fideuada*, which is a type of paella made with vermicelli noodles instead of rice. All in all, a curious invention.

Joan Fuster

The building now known as the Castle of Alarcón was built around the year 785. The best way to reach it from Valencia is by Requena and Motilla del Palancar. Lost and recaptured by the Christians, it was always a great bone of contention. The parador that now occupies the castle is called the "Marqués de Villena", a tribute paid to Don Juan Pacheco, who held that title. As for the name Alarcón itself, it derives from that of the Visigothic king Alaric. Nothing could be more fascinating than to suspect that one is staying, even without knowing the historical provenance of these vast restored buildings, at the confluence of these two worlds that speak to us through their vestiges in stone. To think that as long ago as 1184 men spoke of the "Year of Alarcón"!

Whether one is coming from Madrid, Valencia or Barcelona, one can reach Alarcón and its "Marqués de Villena" Parador just as easily as the river Júcar crosses the surrounding countryside. Situated in La Manchuela, the northeastern corner of La Mancha, its air of legend is enhanced when we imagine the "Ingenious Knight", Don Quixote, roaming over these lands.

You can pay no better tribute to the land than by drinking the red wine of Valdepeñas; and nothing could be more appetising than the local cordero en caldereta *(lamb-stew), or that* morteruelo *(a highly spiced dish of chopped pig's liver with breadcrumbs) that you will also find on the menu in Cuenca and thereabouts. And nowhere so well as here can you begin your meal with a "Manchega salad". As we drive down, the air gets quite hot, though without reaching the stifling extremes of summer. From the sober balconies of our parador in Alarcón we keep watch over La Mancha. But we must now follow a leisurely zigzag route that takes us east and then south, to Albacete, another concentration of frontiers: Castile, Andalusia, Valencia and Murcia, or the high plateau and the south and, as always, the Mediterranean.*

The 60-mile drive from the "La Mancha" Parador in Alicante to the Castle of Alarcón will also return us to La Mancha itself. There one almost expects adventure, for the lanky shadow of Don Quixote will always be propitious to dreaming. It is the very spirit of Spain, whether real or imaginary Spain, that reappears in Lagunas de Ruidera, Almansa and La Roda; or in el Bonillo (31 miles from the Parador), where we can admire El Greco's magnificent Christ Embracing the Cross. *Wherever one goes in this region, one will come upon traces of that honour-obsessed Spain of one's imaginings. The almost concentric circles of our journey are beginning to form widening ripples over the geography of Spain.*

△ 40

THE PARADOR OF LA MANCHA
ALBACETE

WHEN THE HORIZONTAL BECOMES A ROOF.

No matter where we position ourselves, both coming and going, from the centre of the Peninsula towards the orchards or the deserts of the so-called Spanish south east periphery, we shall always have to cross the spacious Mancha and go through Albacete, a place that serves as the knot that links all of Spain to the kingdoms of Valencia and Murcia. Whoever wishes to penetrate the heart of the peninsula from the Mediterranean and arrive at the high tide of Castilla, has no other choice but to stretch out on the cross of the Manchegan arms and discover that Albacete is the natural inn and the ideal refuge for all those who travel across this horizontal, flat and startling geography that gives full rein to the imagination and gives the illusion of infinity before your eyes and even in your thoughts, the mystery of the flat land which is the cradle of chimeras and of the craziest and also the sanest fantasies. It might seem that this land – level, smooth and treeless – should invoke monotony and passive dreams but, nevertheless, the truth is that La Mancha has always been the scene for the bustle of comings and goings, and only from time to time do we come upon a square in a village or a well, hidden in the wilderness, as well as a flock of sheep or goats in the company of a grove of trees, and those numerous farmhouses, that just by looking at them, tell us stories of the vigorous sowing of the crops on the uneven plain; a changeless platform of immense distances.

It turns out to be beautiful and comforting when, after the line of tractors and lorries overflowing with grapes and hay, with vegetables or farm animals, after the bustle of La Roda and La Ginete, you discover that Albacete is well worth a long stop, but not in the city itself. If you truly want peace, calm and comfort, you must go to the Parador of La Mancha, less than five minutes from Albacete itself, always hospitable and affectionate. It is situated almost in the middle of the junction formed by the roads to Valencia and Murcia, when you can already feel the presence of the rural hillocks of Pozocañada, on the road to Hellín or the lookout of Chinchilla, before entering the fertile lands of Murcia, the windmills of Cartagena that now only reflect the sun, or the laborious craftsmanship of Almansa, Villena, Elda, etc. At this critical point in every long trip, either through necessity or pleasure, the Parador

appears, in the middle of an heroic vegetation, like an oasis of peace and tranquility which gives us the exact stature of the Parador, an open space for dreams, compensatory rest, infinite serenity...
Certainly, the Parador of La Mancha, in the vastness of a spacious horizon, of radiant and pure skies, is a gift of comfort and good taste, because rarely will there have been constructed in our country a building that, coming from unchanging arable lands, in the sullen light of an assuring countryside, relaxing and open, is so much in harmony with the countryside, with the extensive line of the horizon, with nature in general. Yet, at the same time, it is in harmony with the typical and popular architecture of the area, perfectly contained in the lime, tile, timber, the extensive wide glasswork, the spacious and symmetrical patio, in perfect consonance with the earth. The building conforms with what La Mancha is and represents as an unending panorama and a room for man in the pure rural habitat, in such a way that you could say the arquitect Sáinz de Vicuña was looking for and succeeded in finding, above all, perfect harmony between building and countryside, in construction and surroundings.
The Parador always makes you want to stop, situated half way approximately, between Madrid and the beaches of the Costa Blanca (Alicante, Benidorm, Jávea, Santa Pola or the Mar Menor) and when you stop to gather strength, and you think of spending the night, there arises the temptation to stay in this immense place, where the spirit sprouts wings of the lark and becomes eager and fiery like the bird on the nest of the fallow lands. How many times, having rested here, one feels grateful to La Mancha and its transparent skies as earth and as dwelling place for the yearning for adventure and the flights of fantasy. Here, hunters will not only find a majestic reserve mainly of partridge, rabbit and hare, but relaxing and pleasant week-ends where families from Albacete with their children, are looking for solace in the flat countryside (it is little wonder that the patron saint of Albacete is called the Virgen de los Llanos (flat land). The tourists, who in this shroud of a land unusually flat and bare, discover the essence of Spain, at hand, in the most famous places, in the adventures of Don Quixote, like el Toboso or the Lagoons of Ruidera. But here the visitor will also be able to try typical Manchegan dishes, exquisitely prepared and served, such as the succulent gazpachos, or a hunter's dish of ancient origins dating, people say, from the Iberians, which has its background in Arab cooking. It is a delicious dish, of which the basic ingredients are game meats (hare, rabbit, partridge, etc.), served on "pasta" very carefully prepared like those of Milan. We also find the "boba" soup, a Cervantine evocation, an omelette in broth, breadcrumbs fried with rashers of bacon, a Manchegan "pisto" (a type of ratatouille), a lamb stew with garlic and oil, delicious and unforgettable for those who try it. Other regional dishes are stuffed red peppers, lamb chops with garlic, stewed partridge, in brine or with beans and, of course, the so-called "village stew", a popular and succulent dish, using the snout and ear of the pig, with home-made black sausages and kidney beans seasoned with local saffron. All these dishes from the interior and having the resonance of being homemade and of the common people, for hard country days and for extravagant festivals. Finally, turning to the desserts, of an unmistakeable homemade flavour, such as honeyed custards, the "Manchegan flowers" with honey, delicious fruits and all of them, before and after, if possible, washed down with the generous wine of La Mancha, this Mancha which extends from Toboso to Valdepeñas and also spreads to Yecla and Jumilla by the paths of wine, oil and wheat.
In other words, La Mancha, this land of an almost metaphysical sorrow and Quixotic memories, is a beautiful and comfortable place for being alone and with others, where one can enjoy an immeasurable loneliness of a unique and original countryside and go by car to places of great natural beauty or of enormous artistic and archaeological richness, from the Mundo River to the Sierra de Alcaraz, called the "Manchegan Switzerland", where towns like Liétor, Vianos, Letur and Ayna conserve a primitive, charming atmosphere. From that conglomeration of agricultural riches that is Villarobledo to the nearby Hellín where during Holy Week, there are festivals of extraordinary originality based on their famous drums. From the historic Chinchilla, with its museum of popular ceramics, to those towns where the miracle of finding a Greco or a Ribera is real and possible, as in El Bonillo, only fifty-eight kilometres from the Parador, where tradition situated the famous "Camacho Weddings" immortalised by Cervantes in Don Quixote. From the Almanza Castle, magnificently conserved and restored, only seventy-four kilometres, or the tourist complex of the Lagoons of Ruidera, where there are all types of aquatic sports. There is also an eye-catching route of prehistoric caves (Alpera, Minateda, Cerro de los Santos, Solana de las Covachas en Nerpio, El Salobral, Pozo Hondo, Casaquemada, etc.), all with cave paintings of enormous interest, some of which are archaeological treasures of universal interest such as "La Dama oferente" (The Offering Woman) of Cerro de los Santos or the Bicha de Balazote, both conserved in the National Archaeological Museum in Madrid, or the famous articulated dolls, of Ontur, which are conserved in the Provincial Archaeological Museum in Albacete. In these caves, one can find not only the roots of Iberian man but also outstanding examples of all that this land and these skies gave shelter to in the dawn of time, as silent and eloquent testimonies of various cultures, from the Iberian to those originating in the Hellenization and the Romanization of the Peninsula. And all this Manchegan geography, so sincere and open like the palm of a hand, so plain and shiny like the blade of its famous unsheathed "facas" (curved knives), having the Parador as a centre and station of rest and wellbeing, offers us incredible twilights of fire and gold, immeasurable starry nights which will be for us like a re-encounter in a revitalis-

ing embrace with nature in its purest form.
To submerge oneself in the infinite plain in a place so pleasant, hospitable, tranquil as the National Parador of La Mancha is a delight and a great piece of luck for those who can enjoy themselves on holiday or during their free time, and of course, with a little money, keeping in mind that for the comfort and the attentive service that you receive here, the prices are quite reasonable. I suppose that a parador of these excellent characteristics, in any other part of the globe, would cost a small fortune.
And, of course, a short distance from the Parador is Albacete, the capital of the province, a harmonic city without the unpleasant noises of a city, a provincial capital with a strong personality and zealously progressive though the signs of its progress have not succeeded in destroying an atmosphere of provincial placidity. Its commercial empire also goes beyond its famous penknives and cutlery and its saffron crop. And once in Albacete, it is essential to visit the Provincial Archaeological Museum, the work of the architect Escario, which in itself, is an architectural wonder for the admirable integration achieved between nature and urban development where the trees of the park materially penetrate into the building and this, in its turn, functionally adapted to its specific mission, permits us, by means of large windows, projecting inwards and outwards, to maintain total communication at all times with the urban surroundings. The museum also offers us a complete and eloquent panorama of what these lands once were as a place of settlement, defence and expansion for the early settlers and the cultures that entered by the Mediterranean – races, towns, customs, which left a decisive impression on our history and which here are displayed in excellent reproductions of the cave paintings of Alpera, the small caves of La Llagosa, Minateda, El Salobral, La Losa, etc. The information is completed by magnificent photographs and there are rooms of sculptures, archaeological pieces, ceramics, prehistoric objects, etc., all magnificently presented. To all this, it is essential to add the three rooms of paintings in which is displayed the evolution of the work of the contemporary painter, Benjamín Palencia, illustrious son of Albacete.
Albacete has always been it seems, from prehistoric times, an intersection and convergence of roads (today railways and highways) that invite you to make a stop at this place of unending straight lines and horizons open to wandering and fantasy. The national Parador is an ideal place for these holidays of the spirit, alone or with the family. We shall never regret taking advantage of the opportunity to go into this land of infinite plains, of an intensely blue sky, of strong and vehement winds, of radiant and extensive horizons which is La Mancha.

José Luis Castillo-Puche

"Do you know how long we've been travelling?" asks my wife, who has by now jettisoned all her gastronomic prejudices and decided to let herself be tempted by every new suggestion. All landscapes have blended into one single landscape. Remembering how curious she became about the language of the Vall d'Aran, how interested she was in Catalan (though the language remained largely unintelligible to her) and in its Valencian variant, I am amused to see how comfortable it is for her to listen to the impeccable Castilian of the people of La Mancha.
"I've lost count," I reply. And by now we are on our way to the sea once again. Our next stopping-place is Jávea, on the "White Coast", near the magnificent promontory of Cabo San Antonio and almost half-way from Valencia to Alicante. In the most comfortable modern style, though avoiding any extremes of architectural fashion, the "Costa Blanca" Parador takes us away from historic architecture and its legends. Perhaps it is what we need.
We are recommended to go down the coast as far as Alicante, about 55 miles south of Jávea. Here we find traces of Baroque: the church of Santa María, the Provincial Palace and the Museum of Contemporary Art. Once again we find the art of different centuries in a dialogue: Baroque and Gothic with the kinetic art of that excellent painter Eusebio Sempere, who was born here. Denia and Calpe are the nearest towns to the Parador. A little further away is Santa Pola, a town officially listed as being of national interest. And also that curious rock known as the Peñón Ifach, jutting out of the sea near Calpe. They say – and I believe it – that at Jávea the Mediterranean attains its deepest blue. There is

an air of healthy paganism here. For this region has been Christian and pagan alternately. Almond and olive trees, carob trees and bays, garlic and peppers – and, of course, fields of rice, for from Valencia to the south (how far south exactly, I wonder?) rice is still the basis for the most singular and unpredictable feature of the coastal cuisine: the fruits of the earth and the sea together. The wine is somewhat denser and has a headier bouquet; this is also a land of vineyards. Blasco Ibáñez brought this region to life in his novels. And the painter Sorolla fixed for all time the impression of this light that is as open as are its inhabitants in casual conversation.

We have come down along the coast again, leaving Murcia on one side, through San Javier, La Unión and Cartagena. We catch a glimpse of the Gulf of Mazarrón and stop for a brief visit to the Caves of Almanzora, on our way to Mojácar, regretting that we have paid so little attention to Puerto Lumbreras. At this stage, too, we find the true essence of the Mediterranean. "Mojácar" derives from Murgis Acra, *the "High Hill". And the village is indeed perched high. The footsteps of Scipio Africanus still echo through these lands. Can one evoke classical Greece? Or millennial Rome? The romantic travellers (of the Romantic age in France and England, I mean) came here and went away with minds bedazzled. Hardly Moorish or Muslim, Mojácar is above all else Mediterranean. "The emerald sea" was the expression Abul-Feda used to describe the "Costa Blanca", as they call it today. Whereas Jávea led us to forget history, Mojácar returns us to it. Though postcards have a reputation for dishonesty, because they "make up" the landscape, here I come to the paradoxical conclusion that it is sometimes nature itself that "makes up" its scenery. This clarity, this transparency, is enough to support my thesis.*

△ 47

PUERTO LUMBRERAS

The first thing that surprises anybody passing this way is the name. Why Puerto Lumbreras? One can accept the Lumbreras part, but where is the *puerto*? For the Spanish word *puerto* means either a seaport or a mountain pass, and while neither the sea nor the mountains, the only geographical environments in which such features are to be found, are at any great distance, the fact remains that the road leading to the Parador (a road that must be as old as the world itself), as it makes its way across the plain that stretches beyond Lorca, indifferent to the lure of the mountains and to the salty smack of the sea from the east, does not give the slightest hint of the existence of either kind of *puerto*. So, in fact, this *puerto* quite clearly does not exist.

Nor is it easy to understand, on first acquaintance, what led the Spanish government to build at this point, half a century ago, one of those "Wayside Shelters" (now all turned into paradores) like the ones at Benicarló, Aranda, La Bañeza, Bailén, Medinaceli and so forth. If I remember rightly, they were all built in the early years of the 2nd Republic to provide facilities for motorists, and to designs by the architects Arniches and Domínguez, both champions of the most modern Rationalist ideas and much influenced by the "sleeping-car" school of aesthetics. And what little remains of them – an occasional triangular canopy or round dining room, or those delightful circular fireplaces flanked by shelves consisting of rows of very special ultra-thin tiles – should certainly be preserved as jealously as many another work of art of historic or artistic value.

Puerto Lumbreras lies in frontier country, just at the point where the road from Murcia to Andalusia bifurcates into its two great branches: the road to Granada and the road to Almería. Thus situated at the immemorial frontier of three kingdoms, it has always been a place of passage – for trade and colonization, conquest and reconquest, emigration and even smuggling – and it need not surprise us, considering the history and situation of the place, to find a roadside parador as the natural successor of some ancient posting house, an inn or even one of those old taverns that regaled the traveller with sweet wine and hard cheese. My friend Antonio Cachá, who is also my excellent and punctual informant on all Murcian matters, tells me that, as in all frontier villages, the people of this place have always shown a certain propensity to wanderlust; farmers only during those few months in which nature permits any cultivation, for centuries they have sought in the transport business their additional means of subsistence, and the lorry drivers and carriers of today are simply the descendants of the muleteers and carters, waggoners and coachmen of yesteryear. Even today the emigrants who go off to work as builders' labourers in Switzerland or to the wine harvest in France are called "swallows" here, perhaps not so much because they go away as because they come back, just as their muleteer or smuggler ancestors did, to tend their tomato crops or take their beasts out to the pastures, while the hard cash earned in foreign parts rests safely in the family chest.

Though Puerto Lumbreras itself has not many attractions (with the Parador this stretch of the road has become a street, with quite a few small hotels and restaurants and a great number of stands selling pottery), thanks to its situation it is the centre of an area well worth visiting, an area which, as its chroniclers have always said, offers the traveller many and varied possibilities of entertainment. In the first place there is the coast; the stretch between Cartagena and Águilas – for further south you find yourself in the touristic jurisdiction of the Parador at Mojàcar, any description of which must be sought in the chapter of this book devoted to that establishment – still has quite a few fairly unfrequented coves and beaches, and even an occasional village in which the inhabitants (in this almost unique in the Peninsula) are at once farmers and fishermen. In Puntas de Calnegre fifty years ago there was only one house worth renting for the summer season; this was the "Red House", which became news in the summer of 1982 because Felipe González rented it for a short holiday. In Terreros, not far from the saltworks, the traveller should not fail to see the cave dwellings carved out of the coastal sandstone, which are much more spacious and luxurious than the many other such dwellings to be found in the south of Spain; the curious thing about them, indeed, is that many of them were not dug out for reasons of economy but as seasonal residences, being cooler in summer and warmer in winter than conventional houses. Some of them have quite a lot of rooms and one may even find "furniture" in them which is likewise carved out of the rock. The best port along this coast is that of Garrucha, where you may still see the remains of a little landing-stage built of tree trunks, in its day the only possible mooring-place for the "Valentín Ruiz Senén", a small cargo boat for minerals which was the first professional commission, back in 1954, of a young graduate of Engineering School who, tired of creating useless things, went off to the northwest of the country to build canals.

The nearness of the coast and the modern passion for the pleasures of the sea and the beach have in our day distracted the attention of the tourist, who only very rarely shows any interest in the hinterland, that frontier region which has known all sorts of civilizations and invasions. In the Sierra de Espuña, for instance, between Alhama and Totana, a place well worth a visit is the castle of Aledo, which for centuries was the bastion of the fertile plain of Murcia and an advance outpost in the conquest of the kingdom of Almería. And it might not be a bad idea, before going on to Lorca, to make a detour to see Santa María de Nieva and the two towns called Vélez – Vélez Blanco ("White Vélez") and Vélez Rubio ("Blond Vélez") – whose difference of colour can still be perceived despite their few splashes of modernity.

For Lorca should really be given a mention to itself, like all towns shunned for their bad reputation.

I'd rather be a thief than a rustler;
I'd rather be a rustler than a friar;
I'd rather be a friar than from Lorca,
For from Lorca no one would rather be.

Lorca, Calatayud, how you both bedevil the language! The popular legend says that Lorca is accursed for having been the original home of Pontius Pilate. But more scientific chroniclers reject this falsehood and attribute the origin of the town's evil fame to the phrase uttered by St Vincent Ferrer, who, unable to convert a single citizen of Lorca because none of them could understand a word he said in his thick Valencian accent, went away in a rage, shook the dust of the place from his sandals against a stone in San Diego and issued the anathema: "Of Lorca not even the dust". Until this unfortunate second half of the 20th century, however, Lorca was in fact a delightful town, descending pleasantly and harmoniously from its 12th-century Castle – and passing on its way the Collegiate Church, the old Ghetto, the Plaza de Adentro ("Inside Square") and the Plaza de Afuera ("Outside Square"), the Cava (a street full of little craftsmen's shops, including many hatters), the mansion of the Guevara family and the Corredera – until it reached the plain and the 19th century, with its pleasant, rather Victorian houses of the Restoration period. A delightful town, I repeat, until the advent of that disastrous megalomania which, aided and abetted by speculative builders, engendered the awful district along the highway, so typical of those years of "development" that did much more harm than any of the verbal attacks launched against Lorca by all its neighbours. Still, as that excellent painter, Muñoz Barberán, says: "Poor, patient Lorca puts up with everything, bearing all humiliations without so much as a cry."

Juan Benet

△ 48

FROM THE PARADOR OF MOJACAR

"...the soils of Almeria are argentiferous, its littoral sheds seeds of gold and has a sea of emeralds..." (Albulfeda, *Descripción de España*, 13th century.)

Like in almost everything else, the western traveller merely rehashes the Greco-Latin mythological stereotypes. This coast had already been endowed with a very time-honoured culture when the Arabs – who were not truly Arabs but rather Moors – first landed. In the roots of almost all the Arabicism so obstinately awarded to this region are, in fact, Phoenician, pre-Hellenic and Latin vestiges. Mojácar is essentially Mediterranean, a typical spot along the Classical seaboard which runs from Gades (the original Roman name of Cadiz) to Magna Grecia. Of course there are some Arab traces here, but they are superficial, utilitarianly added on to what existed beforehand. What has occurred is that the French only want to see what they have already prepared in their imagination: the romantic *melée des minarets* arising among palm trees in a Moorish setting.... Nevertheless, what is undeniable about this gentle Andalusian palm tree which sways in the breeze of Mojácar is that it is a Punic palm, an emblem of thalassocracy and the Barca family, transplanted to this coast at the founding of Nova Carthago, the historical name of the present-day Cartagena.

The highly original charm of this seafront keeps a pre-Arabian secret. This selfsame finely-sanded beach which the Parador faces was once attacked by purple-sailed, black-hulled ships while the nearby Aguas River sweetened the sea that broke against the very same breakwater; the sun that now tans the skin of the bathers is the one that once shone on the comings and goings of the many and far-off civilizations that successively colonized Mojácar; and it is this moon which centuries before settling here in its Moslem waning had already silvered the nocturnal rites of Diana or the pallid Hecate.

And earlier, much earlier – *the cry of the indigo plant against the blinding limestone* – the walls of these Mojácar houses had already been carved with a schematic little figure holding up the rainbow, an Indaliano totem which the painter Jesús de Perceval (the Schliemann of this hospitable and cheerful Troy which is Mojácar) has exhibited throughout the whole wide world.

Dominating the beach, the orchards and the sea is this puzzling and unique city: Mojácar, the Murgis Acra (high mountain) which, according to Pliny, marked the boundaries of Bética, the former name of Andalusia. It is ascended by starting from the shadowy district of La Fuente and going through a narrow labyrinth of steep alleys, twisting and turning over the hillside and climbing and climbing up to the conical top. The entire hillside is dotted with white houses which cling to and cover it like an indigo-and-white coloured blanket, or like an ancient tunic speckled with daubs of roof-terraces, verandas and sunporches. This precipice towers over the western end of the Sierra Cabrera range, which joins up here with the Cabo de Gata hills. The city has branched out from top to bottom, from the acropolis – later converted into an impregnable castle – to La Fuente, where the orchards begin on the edge of the seashore.

From the high points of the city one can make out the luminous Mediterranean, a mirage of blue mythology. Very near at hand is the Punta del Cantal, in the tiny bay of which I, as a young child, once saw a beached sperm whale in its death throes, under a cloud of seagulls. The steep, craggy coast stretches southwest towards Carboneras, passing by the arcanely mysterious Macenas (Mycenas of old???), and, in the end, reaches the Mesa de Roldán, the naked beach of Los Muertos. To the east is Garrucha and the gulf of Vera which borders on the mouth of the Almanzora, the red-ochre silver bearing river; further on Aguilas and Cartagena can be made out, the Nova Carthago which was humbled, like the rest of this coast, by Scipio Africanus Major. Nearby, challenging us with its unanswered conundrums, is the beautiful hillock of Millares. It has a brass-lithic necropolis (made of flint and bronze for an extraordinary reading of the past) full of tombs with earthenware pots decorated with round, surprised deer eyes like those on the standard of Cnossos, the capital of ancient Crete. And there are pots containing amber and ostrich eggs...where did they come from? Who brought them? Did they arrive with the fleets of Minos, Lord of the Sea? Or were they vessels of Tyre or Carthage, commanded by Himilcón or Hanno, which left them here in who knows what funereal offering?

Viewed from the acropolis the sea is a timeless resplendence of silver, pearly-grey, burnished tin, cadmium blue, indigo and sea-green. Thus it is, forever changing yet faithful to itself. And the city, white and also "forever" recently whitewashed. From the sea it looks like an Ionic or Phocian town, and that is how the poet Rufus Festus Avienus saw it: at twilight when the sky and open air crown it with violets like a Greek village. When I was a child (and I suppose even now on occasions), the women used to wear black and yellow shawls, more like the archaic *khorai* than veiled Moorish beauties, and balanced pitchers of fresh water or baskets of honeysweet figs on their heads. As a little boy I heard legends of Mojácar told which filled me with so much fear that I moaned and wailed like the withered old women beside the body of the deceased. In Mojácar there were hidden sibyls and sorceresses like those on Cumae who were able to guide any lovelorn Aeneas to the nether regions where his beloved was.

Nowadays there are pretty tourists, flaxen-haired young girls from the northern hinterlands who come to bask in the sun, play the guitar at nightfall and discover the mysteries of an Andalusian love affair. Do these blonde girls know the traditions which say that the streets they walk up and down actually conceal buried treasures of Moorish kings? Do the tourists realize that they are wandering over the *Mons Sacra* of ancient temples with the rubble of which the foundations of these little houses were laid? It is said that in some forgotten cellar the Holy Grail which the Genoese believed to have been stolen in Almeria may still lie cached away: the *Sacro Catino* (Holy Chalice) which they carried to Genoa and, smashed into a hundred bits, is kept in their cathedral.... What a *bizarrerie* this story is, so French and humdrum, about the exclusive Moorishness of Mojácar!

Laying siege to the city, flush against the Parador and as though wanting to bathe on the beach, the orchard ripens its fruits in the sunshine, endlessly napping amidst the religious melopoeia of the shrill-sounding cicadas. "Prickly pears, fig trees, slender palm trees like those in Africa, grapevines and more grapevines which weave the soil with their green tendrils, extensive groves of orange and lemon trees with golden fruits which seem to need to be lit up to brighten the splendid sun festival by night...." In this way Ciro Bayo, the sentimental blind man's guide, emotionally greeted the Mediterranean. Sensual agave plants, oleanders, rosebushes, laurels, carnations, jasmines, olive trees, pomegranate trees, carob trees, almond and orange trees: all, at the right moment, inebriate everything with their blossoms. Théophile Gautier, while coasting by here aboard a tiny ship's boat bound for Cartagena, felt the temptation of the intense perfume of their blossoms which the north-west wind carries over the waves.

All of this can be recalled, dreamt and verified at the Parador of Mojácar. When everything else seems to have already been discovered, there is still Mojácar.

A.M. Campoy

We return to Puerto Lumbreras because it is on our way inland again. Cazorla and Ubeda. The very heart of the Sierra Morena. Ubeda. Here history is reborn, and it is not by chance that the Parador bears the name of the "Condestable Dávalos", as a tribute to Ruy López de Dávalos. A warrior captured by the Moors of Granada, who won the favour of their king and was set free and raised to the dignity of Condestable *("High Constable"), only to be later regarded with disfavour by King Juan II, stripped of his titles and dignities and, later still, restored to royal favour, Ruy López de Dávalos is a contradictory figure. At all events he is worthily commemorated in this fine mansion, right beside the magnificent church of San Salvador. Moors and Christians are confronted again throughout the history of this building, the first mansion in Spain to be turned into a parador of this type. Yes, it was here that this tradition began of restoring and adopting ancient buildings in order to use them as State-run hotels. It was during the 15th and 16th centuries that Ubeda attained its greatest architectural splendour. But almost beside Ubeda is Baeza, with its views over the Sierra de Cazorla. And Bailén. And then, further south, the great city of Jaén.*

"City sleeping in the shade of a hill crowned by the castle of Santa Catalina": thus did Antonio Gallego Morell describe Jaén. And that generous traveller Richard Ford has also left us his impressions of the place in writing and drawing. All the poetry of Al-Andalus comes alive in this region. The intricate knot of mountains surrounding Jaén afforded – or denied – passage to Moors and Christians alike. At its feet lies the plateau of the Guadalquivir. At times you hardly know whether you are in Castile or Andalusia. It is at once surprising and comforting to find yourself in your room in this castle of Jaén, high up on its hill. You lose your desire to go on travelling, however much your curiosity may be whetted. The Castle of Santa Catalina has an almost womblike feeling. "Andalusians of Jaén..." I repeat to myself, as we finally start out the next day for Manzanares and Almagro, from which we will then go down to Cordova. Castile and Andalusia. And, once again, La Mancha. On the way from Madrid to Andalusia. Built just beside the

village that gives it its name, there is nothing antique about this parador, for it is only about fifty years old. Antiquity is close at hand, however, in Almagro, where my wife – who does not share my impatience to reach Cordova – proposes that we call a halt. The former monastery of San Francisco, built in 1596, it has all the noble spaciousness given by its sixteen courtyards, its galleries and the great central garden.
Almagro is a stage on Don Quixote's route. In the 14th century it was already a splendid, important town, with strolling players, rogues and vagabonds constantly passing through. And the Spanish "Golden Age" of the 17th century was mirrored on the stage of its famous Corral de Comedias. They tell me Madrid is turning its eyes to Almagro again, endeavouring to restore its cultural importance. But that importance is still there, though almost mute. The Plaza Mayor is inseparable from the Corral de Comedias, as the latter is from the Fugger Mansion and this last from the Convent of the Incarnation. All very much of La Mancha, though recently with a slight accent of Madrid. About 14 miles from our Parador lies Ciudad Real, that daughter of Alfonso X, who "fathered" the city in 1255. In 1494 Ferdinand and Isabella established their chancellory here. The city is a veritable crossroads of different styles: Renaissance, Romanesque and Gothic. The church of San Pedro is the most beautiful monument to its past. After sleeping in Almagro (though all we felt like eating for dinner was a little Manchego cheese and some of the full-bodied local wine), the discovery of Ciudad Real took us to Valdepeñas, Daimiel and El Viso del Marqués. Then we returned to Almagro, where we spent the night again. My wife – intentionally, as I rightly suspected – had left some "important things" in our room there. The fact was, as she later admitted, that she thought it unfair to leave the town so quickly. She had formed the idea of visiting the mansions of the Conde de Valparaíso and the Marqués de Torremejía y de Rosales, as well as the hermitages of San Blas and San Juan, all of which we did before setting out for Cordova. And she also wanted to buy some cheese and a bottle of Valdepeñas, "in case we stop anywhere for a snack".

△● **B**

THE PARADOR OF MANZANARES

"Throughout this Mancha – meadows, vineyards and windmills – which evens out its paths under the evenness of the sky."

(A. Machado, *La Mujer Manchega*)

The Parador of Manzanares, built around fifty years ago, was the first comfortable invitation made for travellers along the Madrid-Andalusia road to linger in the land of La Mancha, calmly regard the widest and most grape-bedecked plains in Spain and, above all, remember at the hour of sunset that they are in the land of Don Quixote.
Yes, I said "invitation", because, although La Mancha is the most well-rounded region in Spain, it is also the least visited by foreign and even Spanish visitors. It is a region which everybody considers fictitious, like a scene from a novel, and which they always skim over briefly as if Cervantes had already told them all there was to see.
The Parador of Manzanares is the first modern attempt since the days of inns gone by to make travellers drop the traditional idea that La Mancha of Ciudad Real is just a passageway, a very long bridge between the Castilian plateau and the Andalusian depression, which has conditioned the natives, or Manchegos, to be unsociable with other people and among themselves.
For the sensitive traveller the greatest charm of La Mancha is its countryside: a series of parched meadows, green vineyards, cultivated and fallow fields, almost always very far apart and with no greater distraction than the distant line of the horizon or the shifting and dodging of the clouds around the sun. As Ortega y Gasset said, "we can picture La Mancha as a single vast space".
The long, dry roads of this land encourage the forgetting of real things and tempt you to dream; not for nothing is it linked to the most idealistic and universal symbols of our literature. Even the land itself dreams – so much like dreams are the fifteen lakelets of Ruidera. In spite of being such flat land and lacking hilly rises, in some areas at certain hours of certain days mirages appear on the distant horizon with woods and buildings reflected on dreamy waters.... And, of

course, its main river, the Guadiana, one of the most famous in Spain, is one of the most unpredictable and bewitching of our water system.
But for the moment we shall forget about what the Manchegos and their land dream of, and move on to the Parador of Manzanares – now enlarged and renovated with all modern comforts – to get to know villages and lovely places nearer at hand.
The Parador is beside the town which gives it its name: Manzanares, the ancient feudal domain of Don Alvaro de Bazil, and one of the greatest vantage points in the province of Ciudad Real over the roads between Andalusia and Madrid.
If, after having rested a bit and had his first glass of local wine, the traveller takes a stroll to the village centre, he will straightaway come across the beautiful 14th-century parish church of Nuestra Señora de la Alta Gracia, with its pleasing Renaissance façade. The next stop would be the Plaza Mayor where on sunny days the villagers stop to speak about harvesting and sowing. This is a city among wine cellars and vineyards, beside La Membrilla, the sibling village of Manzanares as well as of its grapes, and close to Azuer and the remains of Tocón Castle.
At about fifty kilometres to the east is Ciudad Real, the provincial capital which was founded by Alfonso X, the Wise, according to the Magna Carta of 1255. A priory of the Spanish Military Orders, with unforgettable monuments such as the San Pedro parish church, which is the most attractive temple in the province as well as a national monument possibly dating from the middle of the 14th century. There is also the *Puerta de Toledo*, one of the eight gates which gave access to the city, an example of mediaeval Mudéjar Gothic and typical 14th-century military architecture. And, of course, the 16th-century Cathedral with Renaissance, Gothic and Romanesque elements and its one single nave, considered to be the largest and highest in Spain; it also has a magnificent retable by Giraldo de Merlo. And, next, the church of Santiago, the city's oldest.
Ciudad Real, the "greate and goodde towne", ordered to populate that area, the Pozuelo de San Gil, is nothing less than the capital of the land of Don Quixote and, what's more, one of the most peaceful cities in Spain.
Only half an hour by car to the south is Villanueva de los Infantes, a very pretty village, the "museum-city of La Mancha", as Victor de la Serna called it. The capital of the Order of Santiago, it ruled over all of the Campo de Montiel region in the days when the Military Orders were the lords of Spain.
The poet Francisco de Quevedo lived out his last days there and died in the monastery of Santo Domingo, always with "the pain of my fatherland" in the best of his works. There is also the "house of the knight of the green overcoat" which Cervantes wrote of, the neoclassically designed Plaza Mayor with its mansions and palaces covered with coats-of-arms, the Rector's House built in a very pure Renaissance style... and the house of the Inquisition. And, rising everywhere, the watchful eyes of all the past events which have taken place there, the convent and monastery towers which used to belong to the Military Orders.
And at a similar distance but towards the north-east is the quintessential "poster-city" of La Mancha: Campo de Criptana. Its streets, hills and fields are crowned by the ten surving windmills with such names as El Infante (the king's second son), El Borleta (the tiny tassel) and El Sardinero (the sardine-seller). With their sail-arms raised in the air, they seem to want to embrace all the passers-by. Each windmill has three storeys: one for storing the sacks of wheat, another for flour, and the machinery in the third.
Campo de Criptana, the breeze of windmills and of sighs, as the ballad says:

Al Campo de Criptana Van mis suspiros Tierra de mozas guapas Y de molinos.	To Campo de Criptana Waft my sighs, Land of pretty damsels And of windmills.

Or this other:

En la Puerta del Molino	At the door of the windmill
Me puse a considerar,	I stopped to ponder
Las vueltas que da una piedra	The turns that a millstone gives
Para moler un costal.	To grind a sack of flour.

And to the east of Manzanares is the miracle of Ruidera where the broad and dry Mancha region opens up its innermost soul to travellers and the sky, so that its 15 lakelets, starting with La Blanca and ending with La Cenegal, over many kilometres at an average height of 800 metres over sea-level, may be seen.
Every hour of sunshine brings a different hue to their still, deep and unspoiled waters: from crystalline blue and turquoise green during the day to almost blood red at nightfall. In fine weather they offer the clearest, most invigorating and deepest baths which a body can have in Spain. These lakes seem to have been whisked to this parched land from some dreamy, lush northern land by the legendary characters in them and the nearby Montesinos cave which Cervantes created there.
Unlike the rest of La Mancha, everything is so flowing and resonant in Ruidera that even its own name represents the sound which in days gone by the moss-green and sky-blue water made, spilling from lake to lake... *oído* (hearing), *ruidería* or *ruidera* (din and noise). Even now it can still be heard like in the good ol' days, in spite of all the traffic, holidaymakers and rock'n'roll. Speaking about noise, now is a good time for these verses from La Mancha:

Dicen que no me quieres Porque soy sordo	They say that you do not love me, Because I am deaf;
Yo tampoco te quiero Por lo que oigo.	Well, neither do I love thee, 'Cause of what I hear.

If the new arrival at the Parador is fond of hunting, he can pay a visit to Santa Cruz de Mudela where, according to the experts, the top European game reserves of red partridge are. Perhaps he enjoys bullfights? At just six kilometres from Santa Cruz he can visit the sanctuary of Nuestra Señora de las Virtudes, where the only square ring in the world of bullfighting, as well as the oldest in Spain, is. And if he lacks time to look at the charming Palacio del Viso del Marqués, or Argamasilla de Alba, which evokes memories of Cervantes, or Tomelloso, called the double village because every house has an underground wine cellar, well, then he can stroll back to the Parador amid the smooth unbroken plains which seem to have been made just to hold up the sky on its distant edges. Here in La Mancha nature does not skip and frolic; this is a land which exists, a stoical land. The stepping stone to...to what? To shadowless edges. To unmeasurable air. To graded scales of acridity and humiliated hangdog greens. A sweeping surface with colours that muffle the vastness and the clear sky.

Here the wonders of the scenery are not reaped by the landscape, by mountains and trees: they are reaped by light, by a light so spread out that it thins and spiritualizes everything, so wide that it covers up an almost aerated bitterness.

Evaporation, the faraway expanses and the illumination unvarying with the sun causes one to fancy that all this boundlessness is reaching the sky. Or that the earth and the sky are reflecting each other. Everything gains something at the far end of the plains: flotation, atmospheric fullness, crystallinity, irreality. That figure moving along the horizon, that tractor over there, and that peasant ploughing are all capable of appearing like modulations of the earth or creations of the air. As the plain of the sky seems to create a vacuum over the plain of the earth, nothing is heard. The rattle and clatter of tractors and carts, the shearing of sheep, the voice of a farmhand or the barking of a dog are lost almost without making a sound. At times a gust of misplaced wind will bring a spurt of sounds which speed past our ears to be swiftly lost in the vastness.

And now, two popular ballads about fields and countrysides:

Gañancico, gañancico	Ploughboy, ploughboy,
Echa los surcos derechos,	Straightly plough your furrow;
Que también las buenas mozas,	For fair maidens also
Se fijan en los barbechos.	Note the lands to fallow.

And,

Ya se está poniendo el sol	The sun is starting to set,
Ya hacen sombra los terrones	Shadows lengthen on the farmlands,
...Ya se entristecen los amos	The bosses are turning sad,
Y se alegran los peones.	And joy comes to the farmhands.

And, when the traveller who sets foot again, or for the first time, in La Mancha and the Parador of Manzanares starts to get an appetite, we show him the menu – also flat but full of flavours – of La Mancha. Perhaps he has already savoured the *sopas de ajo a la manchega* (La Mancha style garlic soups) which were introduced to Madrid a long time ago. But certainly not *gachas*, a type of peasant's purée made with vetch peas or any pod vegetable, followed by crispy bacon; or aubergines from Almagro, an unbeatable appetiser in Spain which is often eaten at fairs and pilgrimages.

Tres cosas me tienen preso
De amores el corazón:
La bella Inés, el jamón
Y berenjenas con queso.

Three things there be which hold
My heart a prisoner of love:
Beautiful Agnes, ham
And aubergines with cheese.

Then, especially in summer, there is the *pièce de résistance*, the *galiano*, or La Mancha style gazpacho, prepared with fried garlic, rabbit, partridge, ham, rosemary, thyme, bay leaves and shepherd's pie.

To remind him of Villanueva de los Infantes he can order *huevos a la porreta* (a play on words: "eggs with onion leaves" or "eggs in the raw") which in reality means bull's testicles, oil, salt and onions. And, if he has enough time and appetite, he simply must sink his teeth into these dishes of La Mancha: *caldereta* (shepherd's lamb or kid stew), *cochifrito* (fried lamb or kid stew with vinegar and paprika), *perdiz en escabeche* (pickled partridge), *perdiz estofada* (stewed partridge), *pisto manchego* (a local version of ratatouille) and, of course, *migas de pasto* (just pieces of fried bread). And if it is wine-making time, the right way to do it is to eat them with grapes. Afterwards, try these desserts of La Mancha: *mostillo* (cooked grape-must flavoured with aniseed, cinnamon, or cloves), *arrope* (cooked and whipped honey), *leche frita* (fried milk, flour and eggs), *bizcocho* (sponge cake) and *flores manchegas* (literally, "flowers of La Mancha").

And, as you prepare to leave in your car or in the train with the visit almost over, turn and look at the young lady who is wishing you goodbye and sing to her, with whatever voice you have, these words:

De rosas y claveles
Y de alhelíes
Se te llena la boca
Cuando te ríes.

With roses and carnations
And yellow petals
Is your mouth replenished
By your smiles.

Francisco Garcia Pavon

△ 64

THE PARADOR OF ALMAGRO
THE LONG CLIMB TO THE PAST

As our car wound past the olive-trees and wheat-fields of lower Castile, I was still thinking about the aggressive and neurotically exhibitionist Madrid which we had left behind. A comment about a magpie made by my companion who was driving drew my thoughts into the past....

"Look at that! A magpie!"

Who said that? Was it my chance companion on this trip or a cousin of mine with his nose pressed against the windscreen who is travelling with me in my memory?

"Look here; look over there...." While children learn they teach us to look.

"Don't point," the grown-ups would scold us whenever our finger indiscreetly pointed at something more or less interesting. Children always aim their little hands at whatever everyday miracle of man or nature their eye has first caught sight of.

In La Mancha I learned how to look and point with my opinionated and judging finger, the grasping finger of ideas and viewpoints.

It was precisely in Almagro, where I am now heading, that on a dazzling bright day many years ago my little hand stretched out towards an image which seemed miraculous and, to me at least, not at all commonplace. There was an open window revealing a dark and shady interior, an almost pitch-black cavity set in a snow-white wall beside a long string of red peppers hanging out to dry. I shall never forget this image of colour, light and shade. It was an abstract picture of Spain as fitting and stereotyped as a tourist poster.

And now it is my memory which stirs me to look. Everything begins to appear newly-born and free from original sin. We are driving against a caressing wind and night is falling. And I am deep in thought about my childhood and adolescence of a dormant and infinite past. The past is just as infinite as the future.

My classical favourites also seem infinite to me. Take Francisco de Quevedo, for example. Francisco returned to this flat land to follow the steps of other writers in the Torre de Juan Abad and to die just a few miles away in Villanueva de los Infantes, thoroughly penitent for his exalted, resentful, condemning, bad-tempered and grimacing soul in all of its styles and concepts. This is where I should return to nurse my hurt feelings and meditate. Who knows if my thoughts might lead me to reach similar conclusions to Quevedo's in his enlightened disillusion. Francisco showed no mercy to Spain or even himself. In spite of all the whitewashed walls and the "infinite" strings of red peppers, there was also a dark, dogmatic and cruel-hearted Spain. It is the same Spain which I dread and tremulously lampoon in my theatrical productions with the same combination of fear and bravery all Spaniards have when in conflict – which is nothing else but the very conflict of being Spanish.

In the 17th century I would have had to burrow out of sight like my Sephardic ancestors deep in the murky darkness of my La Mancha house; devious and hypocritical, my somewhat mystic heart of hearts would have taken wing with enlightenment and the pangs of divine anguish.

What about now? What will happen now if the stage settings turn out to be unchanged and current world events do not reveal these to have improved?

Being involved in the theatre, I can well appreciate meditative bravery, the master of all the stages we shall act on. I am not your run-of-the-mill tourist. The resplendent stage of Almagro is an attractive yet at the same time dangerous one for me. I am fearful of sliding down and being swallowed up by the tunnel of time. Of course I struggle against it. I think about the landscapers and constructors who attempt to restore the past with nothing more than frivolity and a desire for profit. The idea of using their outrages and false appearances of cypresses and campaniles in plays by Moreto y Cabaña or Tirso de Molina comes to me. Are they restorers or destroyers?

The truth is that I am approaching my beloved Almagro with a mixture of resistance and desire. As a stage setting it is one of the most successful in all of this paradigmatic Spain. In an expensive foreign book about the most off-beat and peculiar sights in the world, I once saw the Plaza Mayor of Almagro appear between Aztec pyramids and Nepalese temples.

And now the town, engulfed in a typical opaline sky of La Mancha, is coming into sight. It is a truly metaphysical sky, too far removed from the earth. The swifts, those winged altar boys, are weaving undecipherable parabolic parabolas above the toasted brown towers. We bypass the Plaza Mayor because we are going to the Parador to freshen up a bit.

But..., this monastery of Santa Catalina is enormous! Galleries, courtyards, staircases, wine-cellars and corridors. Was this pious beehive of Franciscans ever full? I will later find out that its ancient foundations had been greatly extended. Between new and old courtyards there are fourteen in all. The past has put on weight in the hands of the architects. But I must admit that they have not done badly. There are appearances in the Parador which do not deceive you: they are real. There is an attractive yet treacherous past beating inside. The amount of intrigues, passions, depressions and self-hypnotisms which must have taken place in these cells! It would be childish to believe that there had only been beatific peace here with so much remaining that we could deal it out to the present and future guests until they are gorged. The true past is less saintly and more gruesome. There are many pleasant restorations which attempt to cover this up, but there are also many nooks and crannies which escape their concealment and remain secretly alive. A little bit of that goes on here as well. I prefer uncanny places like the castles in Scotland which come com-

plete with a ghost. It makes a visit become less plebeian and banal.
Of course it is true that these monastery cells now have hedonistic marble bath-tubs with steaming hot water gushing out of the complex plumbing with the force of a cannonball. Well, I am going to drink a very cold whisky in a very hot bath overflowing with bubbles and see if I can rid myself of some of this pressure of the past in which I am so absorbed....
It won't work! This pondering, like Quevedo, about life and death, honour and broken swords still continues with the bubble bath and shampoo. Wrapped in a bath-towel I gaze at a courtyard through a tiny window which must be a little more than a metre thick – an infallible way of reading the past's temperature. At the back of this very peaceful courtyard I can see some enormous roses nodding in the breeze as if they were sitting and meditating in silence.
The sky is becoming dimmer. I cannot truthfully deny that peace reigns in this courtyard in which not even a chambermaid passes by. They must be preparing the bedsheets and getting ready to serve dinner.
Now the last thing I needed! The confounded pealing of a bell! What does it want? What is this bell, so fitting for my feelings and so untimely for my sanity, trying to convey? Who knows? It must date from some genuine and true past, as it could not have been provided or proposed by any profound tourist promotion office. My resistance is breaking down. I wanted to be a mythbreaker but I find I cannot. I cannot doubt that this is a genuine past I am perceiving. They have yet to invent a stereophonic sound system which perfectly and misleadingly reproduces the twitter of birds bedding down under the eaves to go to sleep at the close of day, or the murmuring of a gentle breeze, or the light creaking of a rusty weather-vane, or the chiming of a bell like a spiritual shower.... (There would have to be an employee to set in motion at certain hours the hundreds or thousands of sophisticated high-fidelity speakers with the same weary movements of a sexton or organist seeing to his carillons and their compulsory pealing.) I breathe a sigh of relief because I realize I am still in Almagro and not Disneyland.
I head downstairs to hand in the key because we are going to visit the Plaza Mayor and, along the way, meet a friend of mine who is an antique dealer and also runs a gallery of extremely modern art. I find it fitting that modern paintings by Tàpies and Millares are sold in Almagro instead of pasticcios more or less patched together from the old masters.
Once again in the entrance lobby I spot a vase from Talavera or Puente del Arzobispo brimming over with those same enormous roses which I had marvelled at in the secluded courtyard where the sun was already setting amongst undescribably soft, rustling sounds. They give off a very light aroma for all the petticoats and pleats which they sport, and seem more appropiate to an orchard than a garden. You could almost make a salad out of them. The truth is that these roses of La Mancha move me. They remind me of a cousin of mine, a great village beauty who did all she could to pass unnoticed, and tried to be discreet in everything she did except for eating eggs with fried bread and peppers. It was a voracious hunger for such scandalous beauty, all combined with maidenly behaviour and lowered eyes which sparkled like those of the irresistible Aldonza, this woman whom Cervantes must have occasionally seen while resting beside a dusty road. She would have been standing by a still pond in a whitewashed courtyard, the granddaughter of Jews, timid, rich, suffocated by suppressions and suggestions, needing market value or else she would wither away, long hair flowing in waves like a river, and who goes to her first morning mass carefully watched over by her mother and the maidservant. And, as often or not, she dies as a virgin noblewoman.
"What's going on here?" I ask myself on seeing many men in dark suits and ties in the hall and other parts of the Parador. I soon find out that there are politicians meeting here, not just from the province but also from Madrid: bigwigs and party-people who have found this supermanchego Parador to be a suitable setting for their ceremony of efficiency and respectability. The only thing missing is a pretty hostess to walk around passing out very well-starched 16th-century ruffs. Are they as authentic as the yokel hidalgo noblemen of the past? Arrogantly bitter black eyes, enforced uniformity of manners and formality, empty and clipped words. No, no! There's no mistake – it's them! They've come back! Tomorrow is the feast day of the Virgin in the Santuario de las Nieves, the ancient country home of Admiral Álvaro de Bazán, and this swarm of politicians has decided to visit it and attend the bullfight which will take place in the nearby ring. Well, fancy that! I am rather pleased – it disturbs me with pleasure – that the past in Spain is still going past. And why should it not be like this? The struggle of a critical writer is to criticize past, present and future: to do battle against the whole world. But I have discovered that I prefer to fight against things which still preserve their identity. All in all, I am pleased that, however hard they try, these executives and politicians do not manage to look like the Americans on television series, and even less like the ones in real life. Their own involuntary and doomed – the Fates have spoken – authenticity calms and charms me. It makes me feel at home.
A similar thing happened to me not long ago in this selfsame Parador. It was a clear winter's morning, and some small land-owners and their guests from Madrid were preparing for a day's shooting, surrounded by a pack of flustered and fiercely barking gundogs. A crisp, cold and wintry daybreak of La Mancha with that familiar blinding sunshine....
Images, scenes, characters.
"Don Francisco de Quevedo to the telephone, please; you have a call from Valdepeñas."
Doubtless it is for me, and I head for the telephone. But, as for the name, I must have misheard.
It's my mother.

"Are you all right and in a better mood? Don't take too many sleeping pills and dress warmly because the nights are chilly in Almagro now."

"Yes, mother. I'm all right and having lots of fun."

"Don't overdo it son; don't overdo it...."

"Overdo it! What am I going to overdo? Listen my dear mother...I am the living image of moderation and abstinence. I am now going to the plaza in the freshness of the evening to chat with a few select friends, and then I shall return to this Monastery of Santa Catalina in which I have the pleasure of a large and well-lit cell to rest and meditate in. And I promise that for the rest of my days I'll not write any more comedies and I'll put aside all of those frivolities which undermine my soul and health."

"What are you saying? Are you joking? With you, son, I can never tell.... They wrote some very nice things about you here in the Lanza newspaper. You see, at home they like you, they understand you...."

"Well, that's just what I've always wanted, of course. I like them too."

And now I am cheerfully strolling towards the famous plaza under the bright streetlights and looking at the many crosses of the Order of Calatrava profusely painted on the walls.

Almagro, Head of the Order and the Campo de Calatrava. It has a nice ring to it, this "Campo de Calatrava." All of the streets look like rustic and stately chambers. The art gallery owner is accompanying us and showing off his town with a slightly bitter expression, while peering at us mockingly from under his eyelids, which I would describe as Mozarabic arches.

"This is my land and I like it," I exclaim somewhat impassionedly, "and, what's more, it's strikingly beautiful. Look at this panorama of streets. It's like a Giorgio de Chirico. Yes, the one that was called the metaphysical painter. And the people are kind, generous, stupendous...."

"Come on, don't exaggerate...."

"And the plaza! Wait until you see this plaza," I say to my friend who has not seen it yet. "It's going to surprise you. There are a lot of folksy flamenco and marinera touches to it. When I was little I had some crazy ideas and thought that the houses in the plaza were not to live in, but rather to store things in – a plaza surrounded by storage rooms full of melons and grapes – because nobody ever appeared at the windows or balconies. What's the point of so many balconies if no one ever comes out on them?"

"You're right! Nobody's out now either."

Our roundabout way past all the monuments is quite long: the churches of San Blas, Encarnación, San Agustín, Asunción de Calatrava, San Bartolomé, the convent of Santo Domingo and the military order palaces, before reaching the great spectacle of the plaza at night with all of the young boys and girls in blue jeans and with Sony Walkmans. But I am still savouring my childhood memories.

"When people talked about the house of the 'Fúcares', or Croesuses, I thought that Fúcares were terrifying dragons which breathed fire through their nostrils, and I didn't want to walk in front of that house in case a Fucar should dash out and gobble me up. At that time there was no Corral de Comedias, or 'open courtyard' to stage plays in. It was hidden away and covered up like a pastry puff in a block of flats and an inn for muleteers. The Corral de Comedias appeared as if it had been invoked by the Spanish Film Festivals or something like that. You know what I mean? The National troops win the civil war, the film industry starts to launch its grand cinematographic productions with farthingales and lots of plumage and, *whammo!*, the famous Corral de Comedias pops up all ready to take in that couple made up by Rosita Yarza and José Maria Secane (who must have promised to barnstorm Spain several times on their knees and act out the big scene in Zorrillo's *Don Juan Tenorio*) so all of their bows and curtsies, shows of wits and falsetto Spanish romances could have an appropiate home."

"Don't confuse your friend," said the antiquarian, "he's not going to believe that the Corral isn't authentic."

"Well, of course it's authentic, but then so is the Municipal Theatre which dates from 1845, a theatre of romanticism with painted drapery and some end-of-the-century sets which are still used to represent melodramas and operettas. It is also very nice, but it's been far too neglected. And that's what I don't like. In order to maintain the Corral with its bullying swordsmen and incredibly strait-laced and circumspect beauties, the liberal and homey theatre is neglected. But, as you will soon find out, there's a little bit of everything in Almagro. It's a theatre fit to stage Larra's comedy *No Más Mostrador* like the Cruz theatre in Madrid could also be."

I, so loquacious, turn silent in the plaza and smile in a way which must be puzzling for my companions. Memories, instincts, the calling and inner conflicts of my blood and race have taken my voice away and left me both happy and sad. La Mancha, my homeland, is pricking my feelings in a pleasant and painful way. I recognize an ancient and forgotten happiness which was filed away in the archives of my mind or – how am I supposed to know? – my marrow.

"And now what? Why are you so quiet? Come on, say something about your flamenco and marinera plaza. See how roguish you are?"

"Yes, I am a rogue. I am half-Jew, half-Moor and half-Christian, as well as half-monarchist and half-republican. I am a Manchego from La Mancha, the land of transition to Islam and lost passages. And Fúcares are dragons, windmills are giants and colourful peppers are the singed hearts of heretical Illuminati plucked from the stake. My knight's ambiguous heart burns as well, for it is true that this uni-dimensional and outrageous Spain vexes me, pains me and kills me with my masochistic pleasure. I am going to go back right now to this palatial Parador to carve a cross of Calatrava on my forehead with a pocketknife and to weep over an impossible rose which I plan to steal from a vase in the hallway. This beautiful rose which signifies all desires and all temptations; this rose which can only be found in an orchard of La Mancha where the sun breathes its last breath and night falls. I knew from the beginning that I was not going to reach this Plaza Mayor of Almagro in one piece. Yes, it's obvious I knew in spite of all my struggling against it. Good-night, my friends, and goodbye."

Francisco Nieva

"La Arruzafa": a patio of palm trees. "An Andalusian village is a living world, with traces of all ages from the Neolithic to the most modern times," wrote Julio Caro Baroja. They say that one can still find, both in Cordova and Jaén, old inhabited caves in the style of those so exceptionally abundant in Granada. Cordova, moreover, embodies all the nobility of an Andalusia united by shared characteristics.

Our arrival in Cordova is accompanied by memories of its illustrious sons: Seneca, Osio, Averroes and Maimonides. Our other companion is perplexity, for there is little for the traveller to record if he gives free rein to his curiosity, Little because there is too much. One's instincts are constantly on the alert. About six miles from our parador lie the ruins of Medina Azahara, the city of the Caliphs. We have been told that it is a Moorish Versailles but, if a certain sort of Eurocentrism were not so rampant nowadays, I would say that Versailles is a French Medina Azahara. But everything in Cordova has an air of antiquity. Built at the end of the 8th century! Useless to try to describe the impression one receives on entering its mosque. Nine centuries of styles have given it its personality. The traveller's memory is filled with images and names: the Alcazar of the Christian Monarchs, the Calahorra Tower, the Malmuerta Tower; the Roman bridge and the exuberant beauty of the women Julio Romero de Torres left us on his canvases.

"Cordova seems to make me feel ravenous," says my wife, who prefers to separate from me when we enter the portentous world of Moorish Spain. She does not say it on account of our lunch, which has been abundant ("bull's-tail stew" was the recommendation she decided to accept, and we also had generous helpings of the cheese of Los Pedroches), but because of the strange feeling of somnambulism that assails her on our stroll through the city. We have taken out our guides and opened our manuals, but to hardly any good purpose at all. In Cordova you must let yourself be guided by instinct.

If Almagro was "a long climb into the past", to quote the felicitous phrase coined by Francisco Nieva, Cordova is the past itself. And in "La Arruzafa" – our Parador – we attempt to reconstruct it, but it is so vast that I have to be satisfied with evoking the first Emir of Cordova, Abd-al-Rahman I, as though preferring to make my way back to the sources through a single fixed image.

From Cordova we have returned to Jaén. It is a very strange sensation one experiences when one so quickly makes the acquaintance of the different paradores. One would say that the principal result of these architectural achievements is a dialogue of centuries: the Middle Ages linked with the modernity that first begins to take shape in the Renaissance and is consolidated in the Baroque of the 18th century, and then a great leap forward to the contemporary age. Such are the reflections that occur to me on arriving at "El Adelantado", a parador built in 1965 and very close to the village of Cazorla. In this

area too, as indeed throughout Andalusia, the Moorish world appears and reappears. Whenever we think we have left it behind, it makes itself felt again with its lingering traces.
"Cazorla," my wife reads aloud, "was built by the Moors, who held it until 1235, when it was reconquered by Don Rodrigo Ximénez de Rada, Archbishop of Toledo."
"The cross and the sword," I am about to say, but my wife has gone on to speak about the guerrilla bands who took refuge in this Sierra in 1808, during the Peninsular War – which in Spain is always called the War of Independence.
We are now about 86 miles from Jaén, which we have come through to get to Cazorla – retracing our steps with a vengeance, for we have returned by way of Baeza, from which we will soon be taking the road down to Granada. I should point out that the logic of our journey is proving less logical than we supposed on starting out. But journeys, I remind myself, are not mere whims of the travellers but unexpected proposals put forward by geography. There have been moments when we found it absurd to come and go in this fashion, constantly returning to places we had visited already, but we soon saw the necessity of taking these roundabout itineraries, zigzagging over the surface of a geography which, besides being geography, is culture.
We spent the night in Jaén. We were both feeling rather tired. It was not the tiredness of utter exhaustion, but something very like sleepiness. And the next morning we had to drive the 83 miles from Jaén to the Pico Veleta, in the very heart of the Sierra Nevada. Before installing ourselves in Granada we decided to go to Monachil, a parador high up in the Sierra Nevada yet only 22 miles from the great city of the Alcazaba. And nothing could have been more welcome than the coolness of the sierras. We decided to stay here for a day to rest a little. Brilliant sunshine and a bitingly cold wind, natural enough considering the altitude (8200 feet above sea level). Since it was now early June, and we had been travelling through regions that were suffocatingly hot, Monachil seemed to have all the relaxing charm of a winter sports resort.
As we had barely had more than a cup of coffee for breakfast, almost immediately after checking in my wife rang room service and ordered a restoring little meal, which consisted of a "Sacromonte" omelette and the wine of the country, an amontillado we had just discovered. It may well have been a culinary heresy. From the window of our room we looked down over the broad terrace of the parador, which is of quite recent construction, and below it the slope of the mountainside. The coolness was mitigated by the hot noonday sun.
After this breakfast we went down to the terrace. My attention was caught by the carefully balanced harmony of stone and fine wood, the basic materials of this parador which, were it not for certain barely perceptible local peculiarities, was very similar to buildings we had seen in the Pyrenees. We had taken quite a fancy to the amontillado. We were now getting quite used to this wonderful wine, which the British regard as one of their favourite drinks and the Andalusians as one of the indispensable adjuncts to their everyday life. The sky was intensely blue, only interrupted by some slowly-moving, almost transparent cloud formations, which diluted the blue and gave it faint reflections. Two couples sitting near us looked at us curiously, and on seeing us raise our long, slim sherry glasses they raised theirs in turn as though to drink to our health. "Your health!" we replied. They were evidently people from the region but, contrary to what one frequently hears, there was nothing noisy or obtrusive about them. My wife ventured to suppose that they were Cordovans, perhaps because of the undoubted gentility of their manners. "No,

we are from Granada," we were told by the man who had first raised his glass.
"Are you staying long in the Sierra?" asked the lady with him.
"No indeed," I replied. "We should like to stay longer, but we are travelling all round Spain and we haven't got half-way yet."
"Would you care to dine with us tonight?" asked the man. It was the first time on this trip that we had had a spontaneous conversation like this. And in a moment we were invited to join them at their table.
"Well, we intend to go for a drive round the countryside today," replied my wife. "But if we get back in time we should be delighted."
"We will expect you at nine o'clock then," said the charming Andalusian politely.
"Thank you very much in any case. Tomorrow we leave for Granada."
"We will be staying here for a week. This is an ideal place for a restful holiday, and that is just what we need," said one of the ladies, evidently the mother of the young man who now invited us to have another sherry.
"Do you intend to stay long in Granada?" asked the older lady.
"A whole day at least, and perhaps two."
"It isn't very long for visiting the city."
"We know," I replied. "But we have to go on to Malaga and Cadiz."
"But it's a pity. A day is hardly enough for visiting the Alhambra alone."
I remember now that my wife had been looking only a few minutes before for one of the few books she had packed for our trip: Washington Irving's Tales from the Alhambra. *For my part, I recalled some verses by García Lorca which I was able to recite almost by heart.*
"We will do our utmost to get back in time to dine with you," I said finally.
In fact we did hardly any driving that afternoon. We left the car only a few miles from the Parador and decided to go for a walk. And the walk was not very energetic either, a matter of strolling for two or three miles. We got back to the parador before eight o'clock and my wife said we had better put on whatever best clothes we had with us. She was quite right, for when we met our new friends again they were all very elegantly dressed. We had an excellent dinner. We ate some ham from Trevélez and, at our host's suggestion, a very good olla del cortijo, *or "farmhouse stew". And for pudding we could not resist the delicious local speciality called* Piononos de Santa Fe *(a sort of swiss roll with cream).*
It was Ferdinand and Isabella who founded this old Franciscan monastery around the Mosque and the Moorish Palace. And near what is now the "San Francisco" Parador (its modest architecture by no means at odds with its historic importance –or its comfort) are the Alcazar and the Palace of Charles V. The walls of the Alhambra, too, are near us. And we are surrounded by beautiful gardens.
"It was in this church that they laid the bodies of Ferdinand and Isabella before transferring them to the Royal Chapel in the Cathedral of Granada," said my wife, who had spent the last few days brushing up on the history of historic Andalusia – though I sometimes think that the very expression "historic Andalusia" is tautologous. Wherever you go here , history is present.
From the Parador, where we arrived half-way through the morning, there is a view that takes in several charming places, including the gardens of the Generalife and the Albaicín. Luckily, we had been given a room with a strategically-placed little balcony, from which we were able to appreciate the perfect symmetry of the garden, without the slightest hint of ostentation and with the original layout carefully maintained. Although

excellently adapted to the purposes of a parador, the old monastery still has some of its Moorish parts intact.

"Have you noticed," I asked my wife, "that the rooms are just like monks' cells?"

"And have you noticed," she asked in turn, "that this is a reproduction of an El Greco? As we were coming upstairs I saw some pictures of the Romantic period, and I glimpsed what looked like an absolute exhibition of paintings in the dining room," she added.

"Well, we'll see when we go downstairs again," I said, and with that we started to select guides to the city. We had decided to lunch out, for our visit to the city would probably take us all the afternoon, perhaps part of the night and the whole of the following day.

Fortress and palace framed by high, dense trees. Thus one might define the Alhambra, the first – indeed, the only – medieval Moorish monument in the world. It is not enough to know something of its origins. You have to go right into it, visit every corner, gape in admiration, wander from one surprise to the next. Once inside, you find yourself in a realm of sensuousness – and I was almost tempted to say "a realm of lasciviousness". But there is something more indescribable in these interiors; it is the way in which the senses stimulate and excite the imagination. Fountains and courtyards. Again and again, splendour. Everything those Moors did here to leave the imprint of their sojourn in the Peninsula (but did it ever cross their minds that they might be expelled?) bears the stamp of perpetuity. Al-Andalus!

If one has ever been to Granada one will return to it, whether the journey be real or only in the imagination. And it is only then that one can properly review one's itinerary. Leaving the "San Francisco" Parador, we are at once confronted by the Alhambra. Not far off, and matching it in its conception of architecture and in its past, stands the citadel-palace of the Alcazaba. Granada rebuilds itself in one's mind, I think, as I return to it. In my mind's eye I still see the sweeping groves of the Alhambra, a green sash of trees encircling the waist, as it were, of the most celebrated palace left by the world of Islam in any part of Europe. To my memory come the words of Boabdil's mother on that sad February day in 1492: "You do well to weep like a woman for that which you were unable to defend like a man."

For Granada had been lost. It is pieces of history like this that survive in the memory of the traveller who has passed through this city and who will always return to it. The Myrtle Courtyard! And suddenly, at the most unexpected moment, the faces of Ferdinand and Isabella, of that Spain that was opening up to the Modern Age, however unbeknownst to itself.

We have now visited the Palace of Charles V and have been in the 16th-century Cathedral, the first Renaissance church in Spain. What Ferdinand and Isabella really conquered, of course, was not the mere shell of the city that honours them, but something even more enduring, indeed the most fascinating heritage left by the foreign occupants: the Alcaicería (Silk Customs House), the Corral de Carbón (a former inn), the Cartuja, or Charterhouse (a 17th-century Churrigueresque monastery) and the Albaicín, a typical Moorish quarter if ever there was one. It was here that my wife and I separated, to meet again later on the same spot, for she wanted to "discover" the Alhambra for herself. In fact she insisted that she should do it alone or that we should both visit it independently. We met again at lunch-time, both of us by then ravenously hungry. We had a "gazpacho with white garlic" at a nearby restaurant, followed by some eggs fried according to a local recipe. Even then I was still hungry, but I decided to wait until that evening to try a dish that I was looking forward to eating: zarzuela de pescado motrileña *(a sort of mixed*

grill of fish which is a speciality of Motril, on the Granada coast). I had this at the Parador, washed down with some Montilla wine, which had never tasted so good. My wife contented herself with some "hake in the Alhambra style".
We did not leave the city that afternoon, but spent most of the time taking a brief second look at some of the places we had visited earlier in the day. For the first time on this trip wy wife did some sketches, in the Lion Courtyard. Night was falling as we returned to the Parador, but we were to leave it again at about midnight for yet another stroll. It is remarkable to see the respect tourists and visitors show for their surroundings, as though in doing so they wished to accredit even more all they see. Still, there is a certain healthy gaiety in the night life of Granada.
The next day we have set aside for visiting the country villas called cármenes *in the vicinity of Granada. Just eight miles from the city we find Lanjarón and Santa Fé. Loja is 33 miles away and Vélez Benaudalia, with its Moorish castle, barely a mile further on. Despite our weariness, which is considerable, we will return to the city the following morning.*

△ 72

IF YOU WANT FREEDOM, TRAVEL

Everybody needs freedom nowadays. Well, waste no time hesitating. If you want freedom, travel. Travelling is not merely living. It is also something else: inventing a life. For a few days, or perhaps a few weeks, a trip can free us from obligations. It leaves everyday existence behind and lets us fully and vitally live life. At the very least, travelling is liberating ourselves from the commonplace course of life.
For some time now we have been putting off our desire to return to Granada and spend a few days in the Parador de San Francisco, this silent and fortunate island of peaceful solitude. If happiness is delayed for awhile it can be savoured better. In this way life takes on its fullness; the longer we hope, the more our dreams become our own. We have an attachment to what we live with our entire lives; that is to say, with the living past and the present future. Or, as Unamuno said:

Con recuerdos de esperanza
Y esperanzas de recuerdos.

With memories of hopes,
And hopes of memories.

This is exactly what we feel while we are approaching the Parador. A life which has just begun, and which we revel in at each and every second and examine millimetre by millimetre from the start. The miracle of travelling is that from the moment we start to pack our bags we are no longer living in the past. We have no past. Time is like a watch which only marks living hours. But it is more than just that. As long as the trip lasts, life circles around itself and changes direction. You live on the borderline of life, but you do not waste away, you bloom with vigour. Each step you take is a future taking place.
We have just passed the Puerta de los Carros and are arriving at the Calle Real. It is getting to be a nice day, and upon writing these words I smile inwardly. This use of the verb "to get" is charmingly funny and mysterious. When we say, "it is getting to be a nice day", are we really referring to a "getting"? And if we are referring to a "getting", who is doing the "getting"? We keep on following the Calle Real. On our left is the church of Santa María and on our right the Polinario pub. The church reminds me of the Holy Week and the torches of the penance procession in the woods of the Alhambra. And the pub reminds me of the music of Angel Barrios; I have heard him play a few times and his guitar has made my blood stir. And this memory is a stir. It is a stir and a strum.
We carry on and see the whitewashed walls, the sky dressed up in its Sunday best, and, embedded near our feet, looking like carpets for the adobe walls, are many tall, brilliant and intertwined acanthus plants. They are wonderfully prodigious. Here they are growing wild, but nowhere else in the world have I seen more beautiful acanthuses. These plants are pillars of greenness and freshness which make this cobbled street unforgettable. While I have them in front of me I do not look at them to see them; I look at them to believe. There is no need to take things to you by looking at them: you have to take yourself to them, and that is precisely what I am doing. Looking at them I become a part of them. I have my own name in my eyes. If I stopped looking at them I would become empty and different. I keep on advancing and I keep on seeing them. The acanthus plant does honour to the street and to the eyes which view it.
The Calle Real of the Alhambra is a not-too-short cul-de-sac which ends at the Parador gateway. After passing the gate, the tower, the brick façade and the moun-

tains of the Sierra Nevada in the background can be seen. A garden of orange trees and rose bushes brightens up the scenery. The end of the garden is closed off like a cloister by another gate and a marble fountain. It is a gadrooned, or fluted, fountain. At about the centre of the façade there is a doorway made with rocks from the Sierra Elvira mountains, with a large wooden door, a window on each side with projecting corbel grills, and three iron-banistered balconies on the top part. As a finishing touch the façade is topped off with wooden corbel eaves, all in harmony with other characteristic 18th-century buildings in Granada. A large part of the façade is covered by climbing plants.

Upon entering the Parador we sense something important: a varying silence full of nuances. There is nothing but silence left around us. At the entrance, in the hallways which lead to the bar, there is a dry and brittle roving silence, towards the back and in the direction of the patio there is a humid and focalizing silence, a silence which penetrates us. The porter, an older man (older than who?), greets us: "I am pleased to see you again". Just hearing these few words is enough to make everything become clear, and a certain trust or, rather, a certain mutuality is established between us and the objects which create the atmosphere in the Parador, a mutuality which clears our paths and accompanies us. When an atmosphere is informal – and this Parador has a very pleasant and "at home" atmosphere – then its material objects tend to help us. And thanks to this assistance we feel better. So, accordingly, everything starts to become mutual or shared among us. It becomes no longer necessary to speak to know what we are thinking. Everything has a beginning and now it is our memories which begin to unite. I am referring to yours and mine. Because something has been put in motion and I believe that what differed between them before has started to become mutual.

During our stays at the Parador it is difficult to set up a borderline between reality and fantasy. One never knows for sure where life ends and dreams begin. This is one of the many enticements found here: feeling reality by remembering and, by remembering, uniting dreams and reality. There is no one in the world who, being here, would not feel this same emotion which we are experiencing today, because he who has never visited the Alhambra dreams of living in it. And it is never seen for a first time. For example, we have seen this dining room set up in a way which we preferred. Several abstract paintings have taken the place of the handmade ornaments which my eyes can still remember. However, they do not blend with the rest of the Parador. On the other hand, handmade objects, because of their very nature, accompany you. They entertain you for awhile and open your eyes. And that is all that is needed. Nothing else is necessary. The handicraft objects which decorate the Parador create their very own atmosphere by themselves without ever breaking the unity of the whole. This example could repeat itself on other occasions. Every time that I return to the Parador the history of earlier visits always accompanies me.

Now we are approaching our bedroom window to look at this countryside we have seen so often. The Path of Cypresses in the Generalife, the white and congested Albaicín hill, the caves of Sacro-Monte, the Silla del Moro hill and, in the background, the Pico del Veleta from which the sun bids farewell to Spain. All in all an extremely beautiful view, though not unparalleled, since most of the Paradors are located in very attractive, surprising and distinctive settings. However, what is exceptional about this Parador is that it is enclosed within the fortified precints of the Alhambra. It is reached from the *Plaza de los Aljibes* where the Palace of Carlos V and the Arab Palace appear. On the opposite side, like an enlargement of the gardens of the Parador, are the *Torre del Secano* and the Generalife. Nowhere else in the world can such a collection of buildings with the same artistic value be found in such a small area. Somewhat higher up, and just ten minutes of happiness away, is the *Parque de Invierno* (Winter Park), on the highest of the hills which the Alhambra is built upon. This is the best vantage point to view the fertile valley and the mountains of the Sierras de la Conquista, the starting-point of the massive Sierra Nevada range. It is a literally incomparable view which one must come to see from time to time. We came to see it and I ask myself, "When I have it in front of me, for how long have I been seeing it?"

But everything has to come to an end. There are lifegiving pains, and painful feelings which are worth more than joy. Well, the hour has come for us to fulfil a ritual. The hour has come to visit the humble and tiny chapel which Isabella chose as her royal sepulchre. When we enter it the air always feels different. We can taste history on our lips. We remember. We recall the beautiful words of the Queen's will: "I desire and order that my body be buried in the Monastery of San Francisco which is in the Alhambra in the city of Granada, belonging to the nuns or monks of that order, dressed in the habit of St. Francis, the blessed pauper of Jesus Christ, in a low sepulchre which has no other feature than a tombstone set in the floor, and an inscription engraved on it." The mortal remains of the Queen were laid to rest there in December, 1504, and those of the King in 1516. In the sanctuary of the chapel there is now a simple, flat modern tombstone made out of white marble as the Queen wanted, with the following inscription:

QUEEN
ISABELLA THE CATHOLIC
WAS BURIED HERE
IN MDIV. HER HUSBAND
KING FERDINAND IN
MDXVI

THEIR MORTAL REMAINS WERE TRANSFERRED
TO THE ROYAL CHAPEL IN MDXXI.

They should not have been moved. When I enter the *Capilla de los Reyes Católicos* (Chapel of the Catholic Monarchs) in Madrid I go to regard the splendour of King Ferdinand's tomb. He truly deserved it and it is his. On the other hand, when I come to this humble chapel I understand the greatness of the Queen. I am sure that she continues to prefer this place. I know that she is resting here. I say a prayer for her.

For how long can a joy last? In this case a week. We must leave now. *Sic transit gloria mundi*. Upon crossing the patio which leads to the new rooms, upon crossing this patio in which the running water incessantly tinkles, our faces light up for we have read each other's minds. We look at each other and smile. This patio was once the centre of an ancient Arab palace, and we had both felt a presentiment while walking around its trees on another visit. At that time we could not quite place it, but now it has come to us. It consists quite simply in recognizing that the Parador of San Francisco has a good tendency for bringing on memories. It is obvious and mysterious. Whenever you stay at this Parador your memory becomes your assistant and removes everything vague, painful and contrary from you. It only leaves what is shared, undivided and pleasing. That is all: it sets your memory free. I do not understand why there are places in the world where your memory always takes your side. Yet that is why one always comes back to this Parador.

Luis Rosales

From Nerja to Antequera, from Antequera to Ojén. We will be in Malaga in another two days, or possibly three. Nerja is built over an abyss. It makes me think of Cuenca, which I do not know, and of Ronda, which I imagine I know thanks to Rainer Maria Rilke's Spanish Letters. *Nobody so much as Rilke loved this kind of town, perched on a height, looking as if it were going to fall down at any moment and yet always proudly in its place, seeming to flirt with the abyss below.* Narija *was the old name for Nerja. We have passed through Motril before coming to Nerja, before coming back to the sea. The Sierra and the Sea. A gentle to and fro movement, impossible to imagine anywhere but in the Mediterranean. Perhaps impelled by some atavistic yearning, many rich Arabs have sought a refuge on this "Costa del Sol" in recent years. But there is something uncertain about the foundation of Nerja. Was it really founded before the Muslim domination? At all events, it was thanks to its manufactures of lamé and coloured silk that this little town became so well-known long ago. When Ferdinand and Isabella passed through this area their conquest was quite a peaceful one. The town's Moorish inhabitants decided to move across the strait to Africa. Then the town itself was repopulated. And yet it always seems to be looking towards the other continent so near at hand; not so near as Algeciras, perhaps, but still a very short distance away.*

We decided to go to the beach at Burriana. "One of the best around Malaga," we have been told.

"Pliny tells us that the tiny local fish called chanquete *(goby) is engendered by the water," we learn from one of the chroniclers of the town. And now we can savour fish again: red mullet, baby squid, amberjack. And again we savour this southern Mediterranean. Behind us, almost touching the sea, we have left Antequera. And now we are on our way to Malaga, having had a brief look at the parador in Nerja; a new one, certainly, but no less attractive on that account.*

"Gibralfaro", a name with two different echoes. Has it to do with Gibraltar, or with some faro, *or lighthouse? Anyway,* Gibelfharo *was the name the Moors gave this hill. The nearby stronghold is almost certainly of Phoenician origin. But the place really had its heyday during the Muslim domination of the area. After the conquest of Malaga in 1487 this area was Christianized. Amidst pines and eucalyptus stands the Parador, on the slopes of Monte Gibralfaro. From its terrace you have an uninterrupted view of the bay and of the city of Malaga, just a mile or so away. A little further off, towards the south, you can also see the Strait of Gibraltar. North Africa is very close here. We will spend the night here and*

go down to Malaga tomorrow. Sitting on the terrace in the evening, with the splendid view of the coast, we write postcards to our children, who are probably planning their own holidays now. They spent their childhood travelling with us and in time learnt to wander on their own account. They tell us that they are going to Greece and ask us for news of our present trip, of which we now send them a bare resumé. My wife has bought piles of postcards and is now sitting in the shade and scribbling away in silence, while I attempt to plan our itinerary in Malaga. I cannot stop thinking of the nearness of Africa, of whose earlier presence here we have seen so many traces.

△ 83

THE HISTORICAL LIGHT OF ANTEQUERA

The Parador of Antequera is a gateway of light. A shower of light seems to pour over the entire city, becoming sweet and calm in the winter and arrestingly vivacious during the long summer days.

But Antequera is not lit up by just physical light, the melting of transparent air, the outstretched sky and the impassioned sun. There is also a historical light which glimmers over the city and its inhabitants. This light is as real and palpable as the other which gilds the cobblestones of the city at the fall of day with an aura of beauty and remoteness.

It would appear that from time immemorial man has chosen this amazingly wonderful spot to live peacefully, enjoy long walks, hold hands and love intensely and reassuredly. The dolmens, or megalithic tombs, in the cave of Romeral; the monoliths in the oval chamber of the cave of Menga, scarred by the well-stylized illustrations of human figures; the megalithic tools in the cave of Vieria: all of these are the voices flowing along the passage of time and distance of the far-off echoes of our prehistoric ancestors who started to make Antequera something more than a comfortable hearth and home. The city, which first received the breath of man so many centuries ago, is, before anything else, a spirit and an insight into life.

When Fernando I of Antequera conquered it at the dawn of the 15th century the city had already been a prehistoric civilization, a Roman colony and an Arab stronghold. Although the city had become jaded with so many changes it was soon pierced to the heart and impregnated with Christianity. And with pious devotion it learned to love the Word which was made Flesh and dwelt among us. I shall never forget the good fortune I had of observing the Holy Week with the people of Antequera overflowing with faith in the mystery of the Son of Man. Comments are often made about superstition in the processions of religious holidays. Here, at least, in this Antequera of love and forgiveness, that is not true. The entire city vibrates with the wind of spirituality when it feels the throbbing of religious faith. A faith which is sincere, unquestioned and devout.

And here to testify to it is this rosary-string of churches, this long chain of holy rocks: the collegiate church of Santa María la Mayor, the façade of which will always be in the back of my eyes; the parish church of San Sebastián with all the grandeur of the Renaissance like an eruption of stones in its Baroque tower and splayed façade; the lovely and youthful chapels, and the explosion of Baroque in the Carmelitas Descalzas, the church of San Pedro, the Hospital de San Juan de Dios, and the Trinidad, Monteagudo and San Agustín convents.

Starting at the Arch of the Giants, which Antequera erected in 1585 to do honour to the powerful "paternoster", King Philip II, the city is a wonder of light and shadow, caught in a faraway past, a never-ending river of life and death.

As I said before, the Parador, with its convent floors, white walls, pale earthen tiles, open views, staid still lifes and serene peacefulness, seems to be a gateway of light and presents itself as the haven of peace which a traveller needs. Because, apart from being historical light, Antequera is also intensely energetic, with the hustle and bustle of its happy and hospitable inhabitants, and the throbbing vitality found in its centre streets, businesses, restaurants, parks and squares. A crypt is what the city least appears like. In this way it differs from other Spanish towns, which rot under the marble cloak of history. Antequera carries the light and admirable responsibility of its glorious past on its shoulders and walks dynamically and vigorously towards the future. To watch the bright, cheerful and hard-working youth of Antequera is a pure joy. In them lie the prospects and hopes of a village which one begins to like no sooner than crossing the first street.

But now it is time to go back to the Parador. When the moment comes to *recogerse* – this vivid and apt Andalusian expression which roughly means "gather oneself back home" – we must leave behind the blinding light, the prehistoric dolmens, the Arab walls, the Christian churches, modern living and the fertile fields. And the Parador becomes a haven of tranquillity for the traveller, who will first dine and then, sheltered by the charm of this incomparable town, peacefully slumber on the outskirts of Antequera.

Luis María Anson

We enter Malaga early on the following morning. We have bathed again in the Mediterranean, by now quite warm, before going for a drive around the bay. A beautiful view from the Alcazaba. Our progress has become even more leisurely. A contagious unhurriedness, an attitude of having "all the time in the world", makes us seem almost sleepwalkers. I think that we have by now succeeded in losing altogether our consciousness of time. The 16th and 18th centuries, the Gothic and the Baroque of the Cathedral of Malaga, are the two great periods blended in religious magnificence. For some strange reason I find myself thinking of Antequera. I cannot get the image of the Virgin of Waiting in that town out of my mind. The Moorish and Christian worlds appear together and seem to blend in my head. And we are in Malaga, visiting the Archaeological Museum and strolling round the city. And once again I find the memory of Antequera importuning me: the imposing majesty of the Cave of La Menga, with its seven gigantic stones. And the Caves of El Romeral and La Viera. And yet we are in Malaga. And my wife is constantly stopping to examine one by one, with an avidity of delight, the pieces exhibited in the Ceramic Museum.

And so we make our way to Torremolinos, which has now become a centre of the luxury tourist trade. We are beginning to see all sorts of magnificent yachts. It is hardly surprising that so many thousands of tourists from all over the world should come together here, for Torremolinos is the very epitome of the extravagant world of the rich of our time. The Parador here, called "Del Golf", is a typical building of the region, with a fine view over the sea. It has all the virtues of a sumptuous establishment devoted to rest and recreation, and gives the impression of being immersed in a perpetual summer. Torremolinos, which used to be just another little Andalusian village, quickly fills up with tourists as spring ends and the summer season begins again – if it can be said to have ever ended. Here you can find all sorts of opulence and eccentricity from every corner of Europe. Sheikhs and emirs, too. We are told that the habitués of this coastal strip, which seems to extend as far as Marbella, have certain characteristics in common: the luxury of money and the unerring eye for excess of the contemporary bon vivant.

Now we drive down along the coast to Fuengirola, just nine or ten miles from Torremolinos, which we will always remember as the image of exotic cosmopolitan prosperity. We catch a glimpse of the castle of Sohail, which was built in the year 956 for the Caliph Abd al-Rahman III and was also conquered by Ferdinand, the "Catholic King", five centuries later. We decide to go on down as far as Marbella and then return in the evening, for we must be back in Malaga tonight. At the last moment it occurs to us that the best thing would be to spend the night in the Gibralfaro Parador. At a halt on the route I find my wife drawing a perfect circle, with some strange signs that turn out to be the names of towns: Antequera, Nerja, Malaga, Torremolinos, Ojén, Antequera. Like a satellite in the distance she has drawn a complex of lines, steep and rocky, to represent Ronda. Perhaps she is trying to arrange impressions in her memory. Whenever she draws signs like these, on paper that she then tears up, it is as though she were mentally retracing her footsteps. I ask her about Melilla, but we already know that, though it is so near, we will not have time to visit it. Nightfall in Malaga, in this month of June which has not yet reached any extremes of heat, finds us enjoying the peace and quiet of the terrace, where we make a frugal dinner of fried gobies, washed down with some of the pleasant local white wine.

Should we leave the car in Gibralfaro? After some argument, we decide that our best plan is to send it to Cadiz by train. Tomorrow we are taking a plane to Tenerife. We will be away from the Peninsula for a few days and will land in Cadiz on our return. Neither my wife nor I has ever been in the Canaries.

As though we were going to America. This is the feeling I have had on the plane taking us from Malaga to Tenerife. As though we were approaching Africa. But it is a sensation at once contradictory and unreal. America is a long way off and, though Africa is much nearer, we shall be landing in the very Spanish city of Tenerife, where we will have to hire a car. At first we are a little worried about the heat, for we imagine that it will be nearly tropical. We have reserved a week for visiting the Canaries and I am astonished to see that in going so far away from the Peninsula (a two-hour flight from Malaga) we are hardly moving away from Spain at all. I have seen magnificent photographs of Mount Teide and of all the almost magical topography of the island. And I can see that when we land at Tenerife our plans may have to be slightly altered. We have been recommended to take a long stroll round this town, founded in the 16th century, when the island was still inhabited by the native race, the Guanches, some of whose racial characteristics can still be detected in the present population. Though not very evident at first sight, this subtle blend of races soon becomes noticeable. It was from here and from Las Palmas that many earlier travellers set out on the last stage of their journey to Spanish America. To the Caribbean, above all. Just when I am thinking that we have left behind us all traces of that Europe (or Spain) constantly swinging between the medieval and the Baroque of the 18th century, I recognize it again in all sorts of details in Santa Cruz. For Baroque Spain also extended to these islands in its time. Just a few hours in Santa Cruz de Tenerife enable us to visit the church of San Francisco, the Palacio de Carta, the Castle of San Cristóbal. In the musical accents of the islanders I seem to recognize a blend of two particular cadences (though they may perhaps be only one, modified by space and time): the Andalusian and the Spanish-American. In the early evening we leave Santa Cruz for La Laguna (a detour at once voluntary and obligatory), for we want to reach Las Cañadas del Teide by nightfall.

The Parador bears the name of its emplacement: "Las Cañadas del Teide". We have been told, and rightly, that it could not have been built in a more beautiful, picturesque spot. The previous night we have been trying to rest as long as possible, for by now both my wife and myself are feeling, and probably looking, extremely tired. We will spend the morning driving unhurriedly around the area, taking care not to overdo things. Once again I have the feeling of having leaped from one universe to another. Perhaps it is the effect of the flight, or of our accumulation of so many different landscapes in the mind. My wife suggests not moving out of the Parador for one whole day. And she is right. She spends the time writing more postcards and suggesting notes that are only apparently superficial. Unexpectedly, she begins to recall places on our itinerary. But I discover that she is a unable as I am to impart any coherence to the days spent on the trip so far, and we agree that we will have to wait for time and the effect it has on our memories to sift the separate parts of what is for the moment a single, contradictory, amorphous mass of sensations. First vision of Mount Teide: an animal slumbering on hard, solid earth. A dream: the Pico Viejo ("Old Peak") and the Montaña Blanca ("White Mountain") are added to the crater of the volcano, forming a single, wildly uneven, almost lunar surface, as of Earth long before any of the ages of man. Suddenly all that remains is a violet, that intensely blue local violet, crowning the conglomerate of peak, mountain and volcano. This flower, in fact, is the Teide violet, and we have first discovered it in a vase in our

room. At over 7200 feet above sea level, we feel as though we were rising towards the immense solitude of the sky.
The next afternoon we drive all around the island in an almost perfect circle: Chio, Santiago del Teide, Icod, Realejo, La Orotava (the Canarian town par excellence*), La Cruz, Santa Cruz, Güimar, Fasnia, Arico Viejo, Granadilla. We return at nightfall after a peaceful, relaxed journey. Once or twice we have stopped to ask islanders the way. "Are you going to Las Cañadas?" they ask. "We are coming from there," I reply. "And we are returning there," I add to myself. There is something strange about the roughness of this island, and I cannot determine whether it is its unidentifiable origin, its geological stratification, its power of suggestion (tropical and volcanic) or something else that escapes our travellers' curiosity.*

△ **100**

PARADOR OF LA GOMERA

THE IDEOLOGY OF A LANDSCAPE

The poet, scornful and bad-tempered, went as far as to say that this sea, the same sea of so many summers, for him had been asleep for more than a hundred years. The poet, wrapped up in his arrogant fable, demanded from this very sea the mythical flower of Hercules, perhaps because the sea is like an old childhood friend whom I am bound to by a fierce love. It is impossible to enter the island of La Gomera other than by that immense sea, Atlantic and final. Godforsaken, La Gomera rises from the sea, from the depths of the ocean, from the mysterious foam that settled here between life, ambition and death: it is the starting point for the adventurer who kept on dreaming of being lost at sea, beyond the intangible horizon, impenetrable and distant. To enter La Gomera is to enter our garden of delights, an enchanted orchard that little by little opens its gates to the sensitivity of those possessing sufficient memory to lose themselves for some days in the reminiscences of History.
Here, to La Gomera, came Palazuelo, one of the most sensitive of Spanish architects. It was a professional assignment that some carry out in a slovenly way or just as a part of a routine day's work: making a tourist parador. The artist was won over by the mystery of La Gomera. Little by little, time lost its rhythm, while the island, like a supposed and scatterbrained Circe, started imposing its attitudes, its feelings, its madness on this love-struck fellow who wanted to possess it in two seconds. In the end, like a volcano, La Gomera became a part of Palazuelo. It dominated his modules, it mastered his sensitivity, making him see the need to use materials which came from the land, the same red land which extends over the island's surface, like a strange camouflage, to which the centuries have wanted to grant eternal life. The red of that Gomeran stone establishes, on principle, its distinctive feature, introduces a different way of looking at things in the visitor, breaks the rules and the formulas propounded by the unconsciously mechanised citizen. Perhaps the use of the red Gomeran stone for the buildings is a product of the self-defence that the inhabitants of the island practised for centuries in order to defend themselves from the bellicose incursions of pirates. They say that Palazuelo, like a man searching for his destiny, walked about the island for some months, wandering through the mountains while he studied the technical solutions to the project. Humbly, he accepted the island's mystery and, instead of going in for signing his name to monstrous projects in the morning and writing articles in the afternoon, he supported the necessity of cultivating the landscape and preserving it from abuse; he did not shout out. He silences his impulses, forgets what he was taught at college, lays himself open to learn what the people, from time immemorial, always knew. He who speaks, does not know. He who knows, does not speak. How, for example, did the men from the land solve the problem of the joining of the vertices in the lintels? How, for example, not to break the harmonic ideology of this landscape that the sea, asleep for a hundred years, has been weaving with the wisdom of an immortal spider. How, for example, to infuse the ambience of silence that the history of this land picks up in the evening murmur. How, for example, to make it echo remotely and distantly with the lost footsteps of the visitor in the passages that would have to be built in this historic castle, because, born out of the sense of history and the technical sensitivity of its master architect, it had to be.
Palazuelo started learning all those things, all those solutions, slowly, patiently and humbly in the months that he wandered about the island, as the only way of getting to conquer her, as the only way for the volcano to accept as its own, the project of the new man who was coming close to her, the little goddess, the baby girl myth of the Canaries Archipelago. Powerful in her silence, La Gomera finally accepted the fact that Palazuela

would possess her and impose a plan on the land that, probably, was different to the one he arrived with, crossing a sea that had been asleep for a hundred years, that same sea of which the modernist poet demanded the flower of love.

It was a question of bringing out the palpability of peace. It was a question of cutting the silence, which like invisible smoke, hung over the rooms in the construction that Palazuelo was trying to put his stamp on in the heights of San Sebastián de la Gomera. It was a question, then, of coming to peace with the land, making an arrangement with history, with the characters who insisted on keeping their ghostly shadows alive. Sublime, peaceful apparitions, spirits of the very history which was to continue giving shelter in that place which Palazuelo would build on. Spectral shadows from history, expeditionaries who here drowned their earthly ambitions, who exchanged their concocted, nomadic dreams for the hypnotic acquiescence that this vertical and inscrutable scenery caused in them. Without signposting, without ragged products of false progress, without mixing the useless remains with the beauty of artificial palm trees.

It was a work of historic reconstruction and of a final submission to that same history that never put pressure on the inhabitants of the island, people who shared their lives – even in their own language – with those other characters who shaped the history of the sea voyages and discoveries, revolutionaries from a whole century of apparitions of land and of dreams that reached the category of reality. Captains, admirals, ladies who, from the battlements of eternity, were to lean out of the windows of the historic edifice that Palazuelo wanted to erect on La Gomera. Characters, in short, products of the popular myth, of the real history that passes from mouth to mouth through the centuries, attracting the curiosity of the visitors and bringing even exasperation and incredulity to those who do not feel themselves to be, at least, catechumens of the history of the island. Like a ritual forced on him, Palazuelo knew of the existence of those ghastly shadows of Guillén Peraza, of princesses who betrayed their own kith and kin for love, of lost honours and clandestine passions, all of this a mythology that could be felt in the ambience and which the builder was to respect, on pain of breaking the harmony of a land enchanted by a sea and a centuries-old history.

Now, in the calm nights of San Sebastián de la Gomera, one feels the peace of these still timeless monarchs, as if past ages had not transcended the years of the revolution of the sea voyages, as if all the land was lingering in the sunshade of the island, suspended in the air like a fanciful dream of Magritte. There they are, ethereal, intangible, the roses of the Gods in the foam that breaks on the sea shores. There, in those passages surrounded in silence, still walking about, dwell the peaceable ghosts from a history which the past made violent, because the times of the discoveries and epic voyages that broke the bonds of a flat world without alternatives, demanded it.

The island did not alter in any way. Not even at the moment when the ill-informed visitor discovered the beauty of the stone that had been used for the construction of the castle. The unwritten laws have been followed and must be respected for the natural balance not to find itself broken by the stridences and pompousness that destroy the presence of history. It remained thus, immaculate, free from sin, the landscape respected in its ideological rules of memory, of reminiscences and of somnolence that require a different reading of its own achievements, of its own epic tale.

Now, in that same silence, the melodies have the feel of peace, the silence caresses the face of everybody who ventures forth in this labyrinth full of shadows. All hopes are abandoned at the gate of this different inferno that subjugates and dominates, that hypnotises and transports you to another time, also different: the time in which the eyes see beyond the appearance, enclose themselves in a dream and discover that reality has not passed us by in such a hurry as the modern calendar would have us believe.

J.J. Armas Marcelo

In just half an hour on the following morning we reach Las Palmas, round and exuberant. Then on to La Cruz de Tejeda, where the next parador awaits us. The colonial city of Las Palmas, which was built mainly between the 16th and 18th centuries, is in the north-west of the island of Grand Canary. At a distance of 22 miles from Las Palmas and with an altitude of 4750 feet, our parador seems to be in the very heart of the island. I keep thinking that the islands of this archipelago, despite their irrevocable commitment to Spain, really belong to a world that was one of transition before it retired into itself. And I think this even more when we reach Puerto del Rosario, on the neighbouring island of Fuerteventura, and we are relaxing on the famous "White Beach". To think that this town is only 63 miles from the African coast! The dry wind from the Sahara sweeps across the island – this "skeleton of an island", as the great Unamuno called it when he was in exile here. Extinct volcanoes, little valleys and short-lived, unpredictable tropical streams. Here there seems to be no history, only geography. Small, discreet towns, which provoke practically nothing of the past of the Peninsula, though the traces of that past are all around us. There must be some profoundly magnetic quality in this island (which has been successively a place of enforced political exile and an objective for European tourists) to let it continue to be so little known, never too crowded with visitors and always with the same unobtrusive inhabitants. They are slow-moving and affable, these people, seeming at times to be the distant dwellers in a world that is consciously remote. Although we only have a day to spend here, in the course of our wanderings we discover the discreet charm of Betancuria; I find it difficult to understand how Mexican Baroque came to this island and took material form in the façade of this church in Pájara; or how the 16th and 17th centuries seem to show themselves here in fragments. An island fated to be the home of myths, I note. Its legends are accompanied by the names of founders and governors of all sorts. Spain does not cease to be an age-old country here, for there is always the mystery of the islands' geology. The trade winds give warmth to the atmosphere and to the surface with its arid, desert aspect, creating an ambiguous sensation of time in suspension. At noon on the following day we return to Santa Cruz de Tenerife, and from there we will fly to La Palma – "Other Island", as it is called by its chronicler, Domingo Pérez Minik. La Palma is the most westerly of all the Canary Islands. And hardly has one landed when the lunar bareness of some of its neighbours is forgotten in luxuriance, greenness, contrasts. Nature would seem to have been more prodigal here. It has proved impossible to go to La Gomera, which is a pity, but we console ourselves with all the information we are collecting. Our Parador in Santa Cruz de la Palma is barely above sea level, on the slope of a low but rugged mountain. Walking along the Avenida Marítima, in the heart of the city, we find all the urban bustle that we had forgotten in Puerto del Rosario. And yet the traffic is never unpleasantly intense. Canarian towns seem to have a sort of innate discretion that simply does not admit the noise of the big European cities. The work of man and the work of nature: the pleasantness of the towns and the changing shape of the landscape, of that great Atlantic Ocean constantly lapping the coast of Santa Cruz de la Palma. Conquered in 1494, the city still has a vaguely colonial air that blends charmingly into its inevitably modern character.

△ **104**

LA PALMA, THE OTHER ISLAND
THE PARADOR OF SANTA CRUZ DE LA PALMA

It has been said that La Palma – so far away from the African continent as to seem not to belong to it, voluntarily carrying on its westbound drift, its sails set in the gentlest trade winds, the closest to the myth of St. Borondón – is "another" island. This word "another" is used to try to specify a difference, the most original identification, the purpose of a way of being. Before anything else is said, it must be affirmed that, as an island, La Palma came first and all the rest arrived afterwards. Its pure geography dates from before its people and their history – as can well be expected. It is poetry, metaphysical poetry. Once it is born, an island can be used for all purposes. It waits to be inhabited, then named, and, later on, put to use. This process has signified an intuitive, energetic and constant labour which, spanning such a long period of time, continues in our present day. La Palma has another type of geology: men and women who are teeming with ideas which struggle to place – or not to place – it at the level which it deserves in the concord of the world. What must be put forward as a key factor in its presence in the Atlantic, with its latitude and longitude so clearly mapped out, is that La Palma has become the personification, symbolization and mythology of all that we other beings on this archipelago would like to be, of all that we wish to possess, the most ancestral symbol of human existence: the long peregrination from the desert to the forest, from sand to springs, from the cave age to seafaring, blossoming almond branches and valleys full of native laurels.

The island of La Palma is, in its own right, the westernmost, the most verdant, the home of the Caldera de

Taburiente with its continuously active volcanoes – a truly fascinating panorama, the most awash with fresh water, the one envied by other Canarians because of its lush plant life, an island which can equally please the mind of a historian or a poet, entertain the most exacting tourist or offer the best prepared geniuses of the 20th century a choice location to study the celestial bodies on the Roque de los Muchachos (an 8,000-ft. peak) with the clearest sky in the world for stargazing. La Palma has been trampled over, observed and pried into with the simplest, most complicated or lucid conclusions reached by so many men and women...Ulrich Schmidl as an adventurer in his *Derrotero y Viaje de España y las Indias*, José de Viera y Clavijo as a historian, Sabino Berthelot as a naturalist, Olivia Stone as an English tourist in the eighteen hundreds, Leonardo Torriani, the engineer of Philip II, Hans Hansen as a geologist, Dominik Woelfel as an anthropologist and Camilo José Cela as a novelist. It makes no difference. They have all shown us their creative talent in the way they took on this island, although it will never be totally unravelled or explained. With its first inhabitants, the Guanches, and their *Taunusú*; with Alonso Fernández de Lugo, who officially conquered it for Spain in 1494; with its insular landscapes wandered over by so many races, cultures and customs – Frenchmen, Flemings and Genoese all chanting the Spanish tongue with the fresh melody of a well-sung romantic andante, and their singular life style in a world so different from the rest of the archipelago: even with all these influences, La Palma remains faithful to a sense of history, its unavoidable geological formations and its poised way of being occidental between Europe, Africa and North and South America, keeping its repute for famous seafarers, good farmers and efficient businessmen. Yet, in this present state of affairs, we are approaching the end of the 20th century without being certain what rôle it should play in a surfeited, codified and equalized society. This very "other" island is subtle and independent not because of feminine coquetry, but rather due to an ontological conscience as well as having an untarnished natural landscape, a private history and the melancholy of its total isolation, which even now is still adrift in the wide blue sea not knowing where it will put to shore.

Our first port of call is always Santa Cruz de la Palma, the capital, main port and founding city. It is a municipality which runs along the coast without ever straying too far from the sea. In the times of the empire of Philip II it was his third base of operations in the Atlantic, after Seville and Antwerp. Nowadays, the city carefully takes care of itself and its Calle Real, Plaza Mayor, parish church of San Salvador, castles, ancestral mansions, many 16th-century architectural showpieces and its Consistory Court which bears the coat-of-arms of the Royal House of Austria. All of these are kept up with the greatest dignity possible in a handmade city, easy to walk in and bathed in an air of peaceful coexistence hard to find on the other islands, which are more contaminated by modern social pressures, the sway of officialdom and the leeching of big business, which detroy everything in their path. Santa Cruz de la Palma still has a chance of being saved from urban sprawl epidemics. The city area is a well-blended democracy without segregative eyesores; its streets, buildings and street scenery have been designed with an attentive eye to chance meetings, friendship and the best human relationships possible. For an outsider, Santa Cruz de la Palma stands out for its living existence, its possibilities, its unobtrusive narrowness, its freedom of movement, its autonomously free-willed temperament and its everywhere-to-be-seen face of peaceful coexistence. As simple as that.

And in front of this rough or calm changing sea, in the Avenida Maritima of Santa Cruz de la Palma, appears the Parador of Tourism, not at all resembling a ship that has run ashore or is searching for a site to cast anchor; it looks like a brand-new vessel in the shipyard ready to embark on its maiden voyage. It is stretched out by its long continuous windows like a pontoon bridge; it was constructed in the style of Canarian baroque colonial architecture, with large galleries made out of wood from the local forests and with a high regard for large, comodious and beneficial construction. This is a recently built Parador, totally unlike so many of the rest which have been raised in monasteries, castles and palaces in exceptionally beautiful parts of Spain. Once inside it we feel as if we are in a real home; but more than just a home, also a stepping stone for trips. Starting from the Parador we can visit all of the Island: the north and the south, the mountains and the coast, the forest and the volcanoes. There is a bit of everything on La Palma.

We can choose from among the route of the volcanoes like Tigalete, Fuencaliente, El Charco, San Juan and Teneguía; the route of the breathtaking ravines and gulleys which goes hand in hand with the route of the woods and their native or imported flora which are unique in the Canary Islands for their virescent beauty, their babbling creeks and their romantic pathways; and then there is the route of the mountains, which reaches its highest point on the 2,420-metre high Roque de los Muchachos and its international observatory; and, finally, there is the route of the villages and towns which, whether close or far away from the sea, are always eye-catching: San Andrés, Los Sauces, Barlovento, Garafia, Los Llanos, El Paso, Tazacorte, Fuencaliente, Mazo and its airport, called Breñas, and back to the joyful, picturesque and extroverted capital. This is the first impression one gets of La Palma – without forgetting, of course, the pleasant melancholy which is caused by its imprisonment and which enshrouds all islands, large or small. We have already experienced the melancholy of La Palma. What we do not know is if it originates in this reality, symbol or myth of the Caldera de Taburiente National Park, which is unique in the world for its original topography. It has a 28-kilometre perimeter, plant life of all hues and colours, foothills starting at 900 metres above sea-level, sheer 2,400-metre cliffs and a diameter of 11 kilometres. La Palma is the only island in the world which has such a great height based on such a small area. Legend, science and poetry have all been unable to explain this one of nature's wonders which is part heaven and part hell, part limbo and part Plato's Atlantis.

While staying on this "other" island we are perplexed by a difficult decision: whether to stay in Santa Cruz de la Palma and live with these people whose ancestors in the reign of Charles III in 1773 gave themselves the first democratic town hall in Spain and have remained faithful to this liberty; whether to pass through this staggering Caldera de Taburiete and appreciate, through this marvellous landscape, how generous nature has been to this island; or whether to climb the Roque de los Muchachos with the will to ponder and try to fathom the mystery of desire for this vertex under the clearest sky in the universe. Or we could always take part in the feast day of the *Virgen de las Nieves*, to whom La Palma is religiously dedicated. At the same time we can watch the parade of dwarfs, the significance of which is not known; nevertheless, they do prove that worship and theatre have never been incompatible with humour, imagination and playfulness. This unfathomable, mysterious, legendary and western island has, perchance, been the one out of all the Canarian archipelago which has best been able to understand the words of the greatest poets of all time who have written about islands; namely, Matthew Arnold, André Breton and Vicente Aleixandre.

Domingo Pérez Minik

"I cannot get away from the feeling that I'm having lunch somewhere in the Caribbean, though Europe is so near and Africa not far off," I say to my wife as we are eating our puchero canario *(a beef stew with cobs of corn, pumpkin, sweet potato, etc.). Or, rather, I repeat it, for I had already said much the same as I sat down to a plate of* sancocho *(a similar stew, but with yucca and bananas), the very name of which I had thought to be exclusive to the Caribbean.*

Los Llanos de Aridane, Puerto Nao, Mazo, Tazacorte, Fuencaliente, Breña Baja... Fine, sonorous names, and with an unmistakable Canarian ring about them. We make a final excursion to La Candera de Taburiente, in the centre of the island, the day before our return to the Peninsula. As night is falling we hear something in the distance that sounds like a carnival procession, but turns out to be the improvised singing of a group of young people walking along the Avenida Marítima. A very mild climate they have here, a sort of perpetual spring in summer. At night the air is pleasantly warm. I discover that they grow sugar cane for rum here, again just as in the Caribbean, and that the name trapiche *("sugar mill"), by which it is known in the West Indies, is also its usual name in the Canaries. But why am I thus constantly reminded of the tropics? For La Palma is certainly not a tropical city. Perhaps it is some excusable conspiracy of my memory. Once again I regret that we cannot go to La Gomera. Another island of volcanic origin, and one where Christopher Columbus anchored his ships and heard Mass in the church of La Asunción before continuing on his way to his great discovery. In later years it was to be a port of passage for ships coming back from the recently discovered West Indies. Spain's dialogue with America is still maintained today in this and the other islands of the Archipelago. South of La Palma lies Hierro, another of the islands.*

△ **106**

THE FLAVOUR OF HIERRO

The Encyclopaedia Britannica deflects one's attention from the 'h' of the island in this way; in order to see what the island of Hierro is, it is necessary to go to the letter 'f'. Once there, you have to look for the word FERRO, and under this heading, in a short description, we read about him who tiptoes across the human forms carved in stone, about Los Lajiales, the westernmost island of the Canaries, the land of the lighthouse of Orchilla, the distant friendly land, where at night the red cedars play their mysterious game of solitary trees.

The Britannica tells everything we already know: that Ptolemy used it in the year 150 A.D. as a reference point to fix on his meridians, that geographers and sailers frequented it until the 18th century, in order to orientate themselves and to feel close to land when they were venturing towards America, which Columbus discovered leaving from the neighbouring island, La Gomera. Besides this, the encyclopaedia tells us that the island has an area of 278 square kilometres, possesses mountains up to 1,500 metres high, has a mist in the capital, Valverde, and twelve years ago had a population of 5,503 inhabitants.

The encyclopaedias cannot say what there really is on the land because books live by words and the land lives by smells, it endures thanks to the flavour. It is impossible for any book to convey the smell of Hierro when one approaches the harbour of la Estaca and sees before one the black iron mass of the island that has the best fish soup in the world, which is accompanied by well-cooked rice; it is splendidly made in another harbour, much less ambitious and with a name even more memorable: La Restinga. Neither encyclopaedias nor conversation can convey the nostalgia for the meseta, the smell of the sea when it crashes against those black rocks, the final point of the wash that descends from Los Lajiales in search of a water that in the afternoon is pink and at night is moon blue and during the day is blue. It offers a full variety of marine life, the tastiest and most difficult to catch fish in the world, the old frisky and scaly female that guards between the folds of her scales, the most alive flavour of the rocks to which this most worthy fish clings. Neither can the encyclopaedia describe the succulent fruit that grows in the centre of the island, and which offers itself freely, exactly like fruit generally offers itself, to the traveller who wishes to take it in the middle of the woods where fig trees grow for the solace of the tired and the delight of the hungry, for the almost circus-like spectacle for the children: while the adults jump up to reach the branches of the green-white fig trees in search of the fruit that, like the air, is given away free in this humid, dry, misty and sunny land.

The encyclopaedias cannot say anything of the romantic spectacle of those roughly made routes along which the traveller ventures to find at the end of the journey, the most mysterious wood in the world: the forest of the red cedars, age-old arboreal figures that are there like a treasure of vegetation and archaeology, pointing towards the sea, like museum pieces, like pictures that have jumped out of a Van Gogh canvas and stand out calmly without embarrassment. There is also the wisdom of the trees that have lived next to the sea, in the middle of the ocean, with its face turned towards the lighthouse of Orchilla, watching all the sailors pass by, distant and fearful where here they make the last sign of the cross close to land. Mysterious trees which turn right around, with their dry branches and dolorous appearance, to stare as you abandon such a desolate landscape and then turn back again to contemplate the sea that you have left because there is also an echo there in a different way, as if it established a dialogue with what lay beyond the depths of the Atlantic.

On the way back, some goats, a few sheep, a peasant or an inevitable character in the island – José Padrón Machín – place you again on the land and offer you, in the case of the latter, figs from the wild fig trees. It shows you the once-seen-never-forgotten face of the lizard of Salmor or it makes you ascend by the green roads towards the Gulf area to see the place where a boat once set off that never reached the harbour, to observe the freshwater springs of Sabinosa, where the cripples sometimes found rest and where today the salt water continues to be a source of hope for hundreds of people who come every summer to look for solace for their suffering among the splendours of that area of Hierro. They offer you cheesecakes accompanied by milk, or they give you cheese, and you have it all as if it came from the centre of the earth, as if it had been cooked with the heat from lava, in the middle of the shapes of Los Lajiales, on a stormy night, when the island still was not completely formed. Although it is daylight, everything is mysterious in Hierro, and for this reason we walk towards the look-out point from which the parador of Hierro can be seen and, in front of this unpolluted figure that lies below, you wonder if you are not facing the dry, white presence of a ghostlike piece of real estate, which it was for years. It was a ghost-like property, a place which you could not get access to thanks to a combination of circumstances among which bureaucracy and its geographical position stand out. And it was true, you would go across to the other side of the island, trying to arrive at the white parador and you would find that tradition had converted it into something inaccessible. The jutting slate of Hierro appeared to be on the point of falling on your car, or on your head, but it was not anything, nothing ever seemed to happen. For years, the parador was an impossible place for the traveller to reach. Today, its physiognomy discovered, made usable for the benefit of walkers and a rest place for those who formerly could not think of the island as a complete refuge, that parador stands out as the quintessence of a flavour: the flavour of Hierro.

But the parador would not be anything if it was not surrounded by the mysterious and friendly island that at the end of the day offers you the rosy light of the sea and the white expanse of tablecloths, like gold in clothes, where those that today come to this establishment are seated. Somerset Maugham could not see this but it would have been an excellent source for his enthusiastic descriptions of Spanish paradors. Before its difficult inauguration it would have been a theme for H.P. Lovecraft. Today it is a theme of tranquility for those that consider a traveller's biography incomplete without previously having sampled, in the middle of that experience, the flavour of Hierro.

Juan Cruz Ruiz

The paradores corresponding to the first part of our itinerary appear in this volume.

△ 1 Parador del Valle de Arán. Viella. (Lérida).

△ 4 Parador de Ordesa. (Huesca).

△ 6 Parador "Monte Perdido". Bielsa. (Huesca).

△ 10 Parador "Don Gaspar de Portolá". Arties. (Lérida).

△ 15 Parador de Seo de Urgel. Seo de Urgel. (Lérida).

△ 17 Parador "Duques de Cardona". Cardona. (Barcelona).

△ 20 Parador de Vich. Vich. (Barcelona).

△ 23 Parador "Costa Brava". Aiguablava. (Gerona).

△ 26 Parador "Castillo de la Zuda". Tortosa. (Tarragona).

△ 28 Parador "Costa del Azahar". Benicarló. (Castellón).

△ 30 Parador "La Concordia". Alcañiz. (Teruel).

△ 32 Parador de Teruel. Teruel.

△ 35 Parador "Luis Vives". El Saler. (Valencia).

△ 37 Parador "Marqués de Villena". Alarcón. (Cuenca).

△ 40 Parador "La Mancha". Albacete.

△ 43 Parador "Costa Blanca". Jávea. (Alicante).

△ 47 Parador Puerto Lumbreras. Puerto Lumbreras. (Murcia).

△ 48 Parador "Reyes Católicos". Mojacar. (Almería).

△ 52 Parador "El Adelantado". Cazorla. (Jaén).

△ 57 Parador "Condestable Dávalos". Úbeda. (Jaén).

△● A Parador de Bailén. (Jaén).

△● B Parador de Manzanares. Manzanares. (Ciudad Real).

△ 64 Parador de Almagro. Almagro. (Ciudad Real).

△ 66 Parador "Castillo de Santa Catalina". Jaén.

△ 70 Parador "La Arruzafa". Cordova.

△ 72 Parador "San Francisco". Granada.

△ 76 Parador de Sierra Nevada. Monachil. (Granada).

△ 79 Parador de Nerja. Nerja. Málaga.

△ 83 Parador de Antequera. Antequera. (Málaga).

△ 86 Parador de "Juanar". Ojén. (Málaga).

△ 88 Parador "Del Golf". Torremolinos. (Málaga).

△ 90 Parador de "Gibralfaro". Málaga.

△ 94 Parador "Don Pedro de Estopiñán". Melilla.

△ 97 Parador de las Cañadas del Teide. (Tenerife)

△ 100 Parador "Conde de la Gomera". (La Gomera).

△ 104 Parador de Santa Cruz de la Palma. (Isla de la Palma).

△ 106 Parador de Hierro. (Hierro).

△ 110 Parador Cruz de Tejeda. (Gran Canaria).

△ 114 Parador de Fuerteventura. Puerto del Rosario. (Fuerteventura).

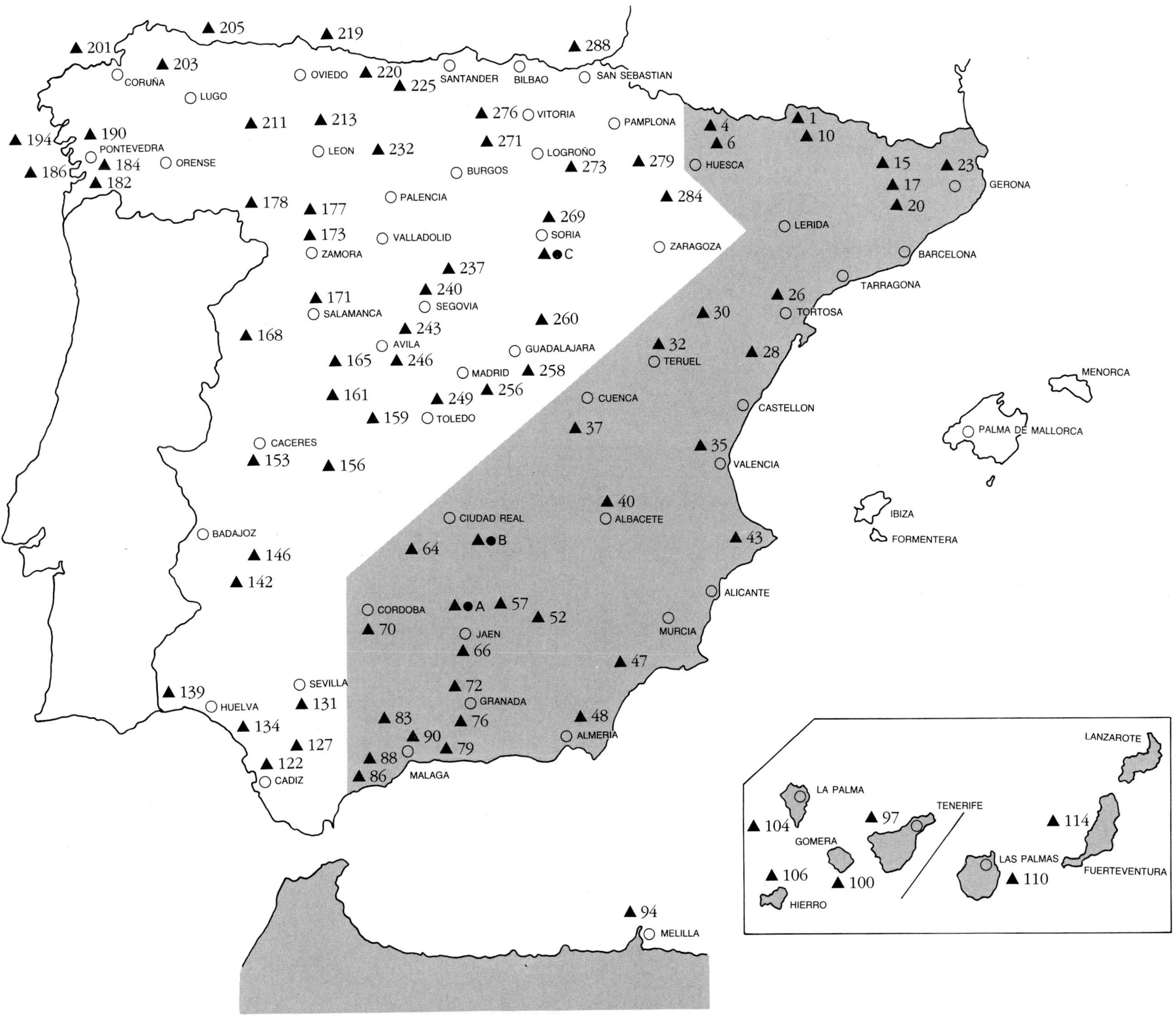

CORUÑA
LUGO
OVIEDO
SANTANDER
BILBAO
SAN SEBASTIAN
VITORIA
PAMPLONA
PONTEVEDRA
ORENSE
LEON
LOGROÑO
BURGOS
HUESCA
GERONA
PALENCIA
LERIDA
SORIA
VALLADOLID
ZAMORA
ZARAGOZA
BARCELONA
TARRAGONA
SALAMANCA
SEGOVIA
TORTOSA
AVILA
GUADALAJARA
TERUEL
MADRID
MENORCA
CUENCA
CASTELLON
TOLEDO
PALMA DE MALLORCA
CACERES
VALENCIA
IBIZA
CIUDAD REAL
ALBACETE
FORMENTERA
BADAJOZ
ALICANTE
CORDOBA
MURCIA
JAEN
SEVILLA
GRANADA
HUELVA
ALMERIA
CADIZ
MALAGA
MELILLA
LANZAROTE
LA PALMA
TENERIFE
GOMERA
LAS PALMAS
FUERTEVENTURA
HIERRO

△4

△ 6

△7

8

9

△ 10

14

△ 15

△ 16

△ 17

△ 18

△ 20

△ 21

23

△ 24

△ 26

△ 27

△ 28

△ 30

△ 32

△ 33

△ 35

37

△ 40

△ 43

△ 44

△ 47

△ 48

△ 49

△ 52

△ 57

△ 58

63 △ 64

△ 66

67

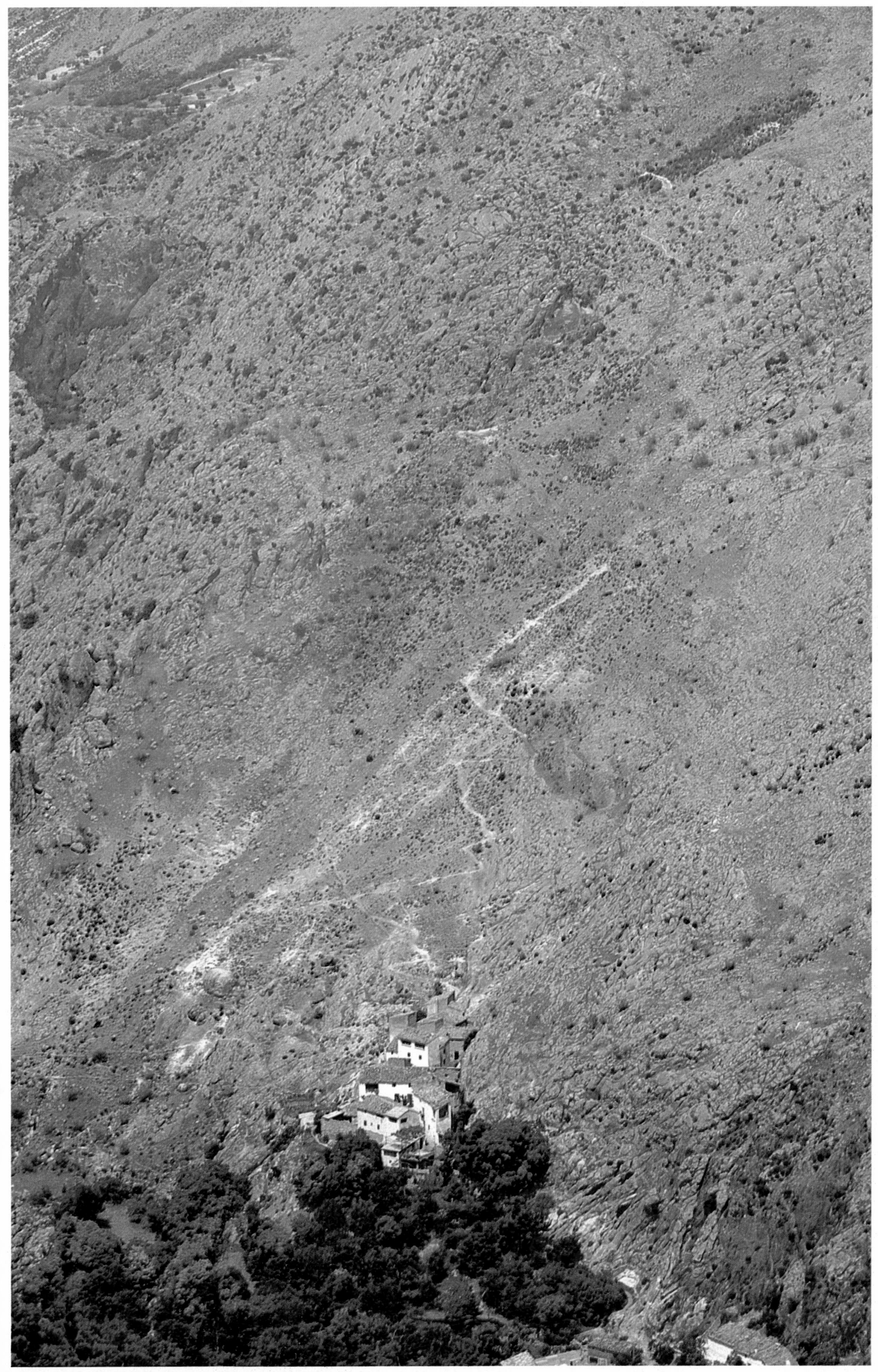

BAILIO

△ 70

△ 72

△ 73

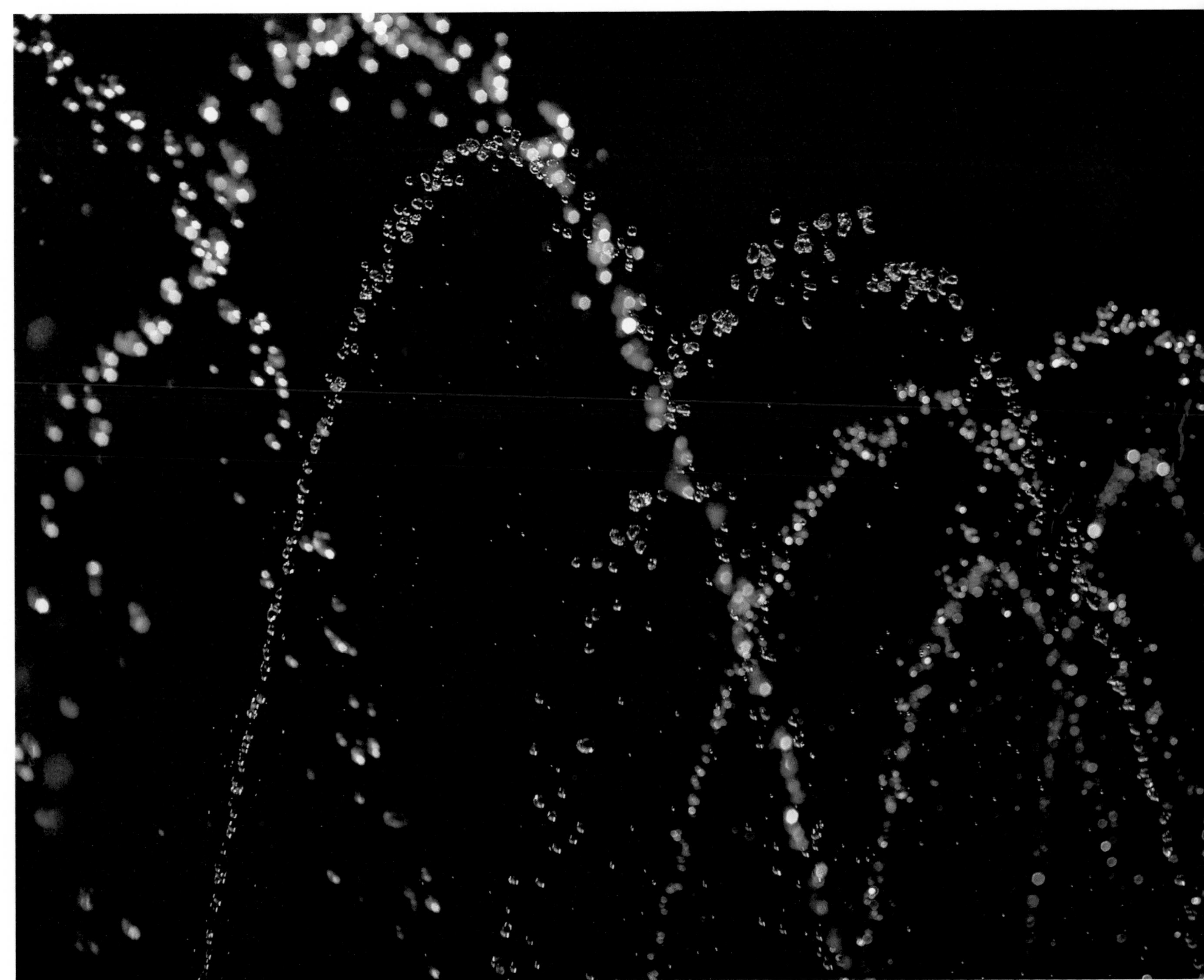

△ 76

△ 79

△ 83

△ 84

△ 88

△ 90

△ 91

△ 95

△ 97

△ 100

△ 104

△ 110

△ 114

115

116

PHOTO CAPTIONS

△ 1 The Val d'Arán on the preceding page. The Parador of Viella in the foreground and Pyrenean scenery in the background. A large room in the Parador.

2 Snow-covered mountains in the Pyrenees of Lérida.

3 Baqueira-Beret: the winter resort with the most important social life in Spain (Lérida).

△ 4 The Ordesa Refugio, Torla, in the Pyrenees of Huesca.

5 The National Park of Ordesa.

△ 6 The Monte Perdido Parador in the midst of the Pyrenees of Huesca.

△ 7 Rooms with a subtle Pyrenean style in the Parador of Bielsa.

8 A wide corner of the National Park of Ordesa (Huesca).

9 A view of lake San Mauricio – a haven of peace in the Pyrenees of Lérida.

△ 10 The Parador of Arties and some of its modern and elegant rooms.

△ 11 The reception desk and dining-room in the Parador of Arties.

12 Ortó near Seo de Urgel and its awesome Pyrenean greenery.

13 The church of Sant Climent de Taüll (Lérida).

14 A view of the historic town of Seo de Urgel.

△ 15 The Parador of Seo de Urgel. This Parador was constructed over the site of the 14th-century convent church of Santo Domingo – the remains of the cloister and temple have been duly restored.

△ 16 Beautiful and spacious rooms of the Seo de Urgel Parador. Its swimming pool designed in a strikingly modern style.

△ 17 A view of the Parador Duques de Cardona in the province of Barcelona; the village of Cardona and the Parador in the background. The castle which Enrique of Aragón the Duque de Cardona had built in the year 1600.

△ 18 Architectural highlights of the village of Cardona and some rooms in its Parador.

△ 19 Dining-rooms, sitting rooms and the inside courtyard of the Parador Duques de Cardona.

△ 20 A general view of the Parador of Vic and the reservoir of Sau.

△ 21 The interior of the magnificent Parador of Vic.

22 A picturesque scene of the market of Vic.

△ 23 Aiguablava on the Costa Brava and its Parador in the background.

△ 24 A panoramic view and highlights of the Parador of Aiguablava and its beach.

25 A view of the Costa Brava: Llafranch in the foreground and Calella de Palafrugell in the background.

△ 26 Views of the Tortosa Parador, the *Zuda* Castle in the province of Tarragona. It is located on the hilltop which the prehistoric tribe of Ilercavons first settled. In the 10th century the Romans built an acropolis here.

△ 27 Rooms and dining-room of the Zuda Parador Castle. A night view of Tortosa.

△ 28 The Parador Costa de Azahar in Benicarló and the view from its garden.

29 A view of Peñíscola, a welcoming summer resort.

△ 30 View of the Parador of Alcañiz (Teruel). A beautiful view of its interior corridors and gardens. It was constructed during the reconquest of Spain from the Moors (12th century); later King Alfonso II bestowed it on the Order of Calatrava in 1179.

31 The Organos de Montoro (Teruel).

△ 32 A view of the Parador of Teruel.

△ 33 The entranceway to the Parador of Teruel.

34 Sunset over the Albufera (Valencia).

△ 35 Scenes of the Parador Luis Vives in the Saler district (Valencia). Its golf course and main entrance.

36 The village of Belmonte and its ramparts, in the province of Cuenca.

△ 37 A sensational view of the Parador Marqués de Villena in Alarcón (Cuenca). Originally Arabic, it was built by Alarco in the 8th century and reconstructed by the Marqués de Villena in the 14th century.

△ 38 Rooms in the Castilian tradition in the Parador of Alarcón.

39 The silhouette of Albacete as seen from its wide fields.

△ 40 The Parador of Albacete and some interior views of it.

41 A palm grove of Alicante, on the way to Guadalest.

42 A charming seascape in Guadalest (Alicante).

△ 43-44 Views of the Parador of Jávea with a quay and seaside gardens.

45 A characteristic Mediterranean landscape, seen from the Mirador of Benidorm (Alicante).

46 The traditional procession of the Virgen del Carmen, the patron of fishermen, in Murcia.

△ 47 An aerial view of the entrance and ceramics market in the Parador of Puerto Lumbreras (Murcia).

△ 48 A view of Mojácar and rooms in the Parador Reyes Católicos.

△ 49 Details of the Parador Reyes Católicos: sitting rooms, the dining-room and gardens.

50 Beaches in the locality of Aguilas and the "Cuatro Calas" (Murcia).

51 The contrasts of a countryside: the National Game Reserve of Cazorla y Segura in the province of Jaen and fields of Almería.

△ 52 The Parador in the Sierra de Cazorla.

53 The Tranco reservoir in the Sierra de Cazorla.

54 Fauna of the Sierra de Cazorla.

55 The city of Cazorla perched on the sierra which bears its name.

56 A view from the distorted rocks of Cazorla.

△ 57 A view of Ubeda from its Parador Condestable Dávalos. The Palace of Dean Ortega: this building dates back to the 16th century, although it was totally renovated in the 17th century.

△ 58 Breathtaking photographs of the interior of the Parador Condestable Dávalos.

59 A sunset in Daimiel (Ciudad Real).

60 A view of Baños de la Encina.

61 A street in Almansa and the castle in the background (Albacete).

62 A view of Campo de Criptana.

63 △ 64 Views of Almagro, the city, the entranceway and interiors of the Parador.

△ 65 The Parador of Almagro: interior views and details of its surroundings in the province of Ciudad Real. This Parador was built over the ancient convent of San Francisco which the Dávila de la Cueva family built in 1596.

△ 66 The Castillo de Santa Catalina Parador in Jaén. It was constructed by order of King Alhamar, who also started the building of the Alhambra in Granada. Fernando III the Saint conquered it and had it modified to become a residence of the Castilian Monarchs.

△ 67 The multicoloured town centre of Jaén and its olive groves. In the preceding pages, the Parador, some interior views of it and, lastly, a view of Belenda.

68 A charming street in Cordova.

69 The Mosque of Cordova – a splendid reminder of the past.

△ 70 The Arruzafa Parador in Cordova.

71 Fields of Alpujarra (Granada).

△ 72 The discrete and beautiful Parador of San Francisco in Granada. It is an ancient mosque and Arab palace which was reconstructed by Yusuf I of Granada between 1332 and 1334. The Catholic Monarchs converted it into a convent in the 16th century.

△ 73 Interior details of the Parador of Granada.

74 Sparkling play of light and water in the Alhambra.

△ 75 A magnificent exterior view of the Alhambra. Highlights of the Alhambra and the Albaicín; two jewels of Granada.

△ 76 The Sierra Nevada mountains seen from the Veleta, a view of the Parador Sierra Nevada and its nearby ski slopes.

77-78 General views of the Alpujarra (Granada) and the Río Verde valley.

△ 79 The Parador of Nerja (Málaga) near the delightful scenic viewpoint called the "Balcony of Europe".

80 A fascinating view of the caves of Nerja.

81 The pass of the Gaitanes (Málaga).

82 Antequera is a characteristic Andalusian village.

△ 83 A view of the modern Parador in Antequera.

△ 84 Rooms of the Parador of Antequera.

85 The haughty city of Ronda.

△ 86 The Parador Juanar in Ojén on the Ronda mountain range (Málaga).

87 A view of Ojén.

△ 88 The Parador Del Golf in Torremolinos: luxury and discretion.

89 △ 90 Scenes of Málaga and its Parador Gibralfaro.

△ 91 The gardens of the Parador Gibralfaro (Málaga).

92 Puerto Banus', a recreational port in Málaga province.

93 The Juan Sebastián El Cano, school-ship of the Spanish Navy, anchored at Melilla. A view of the city.

△ 94-95 Melilla, the Don Pedro de Estopiñán Parador and the Lobera Park.

96 Tenerife seen from Gomera island.

△ 97 The Parador Las Canadas del Teide on Tenerife. An impressive geological setting of the area.

98 A view of Bajamar in the valley of Orotava. (Tenerife).

99 Surfing at Tenerife.

△ 100 The Parador San Sebastián on Gomera island and some of its rooms.

101 A typical Canarian patio. The Carta Palace in Santa Cruz de Tenerife can be seen in the photograph.

102 The silhouettes of Gomera and Hierro islands as seen from La Palma.

103 Caldera de Taburiente on the island of La Palma.

△ 104 An exterior view of the Parador of Santa Cruz de la Palma.

105 Scenery on the island of La Palma.

△ 106 The Parador on the island of Hierro in the Canaries.

107 Picturesque flower market and scenery on the island of Hierro.

108 A view of the unusual geological formations on the island of Hierro.

109 Dunes of Maspalomas on Gran Canaria.

△ 110 The Parador Cruz de Tejeda on Gran Canaria.

111 Mountain landscapes around the Cruz de Tejeda.

112 Arucas on Las Palmas.

113 The beaches of Fuerteventura.

△ 114 Blanca beach and the Parador of Fuerteventura in Puerto del Rosario.

115 Details of the well taken care of and almost primitive architecture of Fuerteventura.

116 Another unusual Canarian landscape.

117 A view of the islet called Graciosa seen from the vantage point of Lanzarote.

118 The customary camelback ride.

119 Aria on Lanzarote.

INDEX OF TEXTS

PHOTOGRAPHERS

A.G.E. Fotosotck.
Altair
Amalio
Arnaiz
Hermanos Blasi
Castuesa
Catalá Roca
Ciganovic
Dallet
R.G. Everts
F.I.S.A.
F3; S.A.
Garrido
Herraez
Herrero
I.C.F.
Imagen Fotógrafos
Kindel
Lamarca
Larrea
Foto Lax
J. de Lizaur
Masats
Mautheer
Monterry
Muller
Onieva
Ontañón
Oronoz
Paisajes Españoles
Perdomo
Rickenback
Roig Forn
Rojas
Signier
S.O.F.
Soria
E. de la Vega
Verdugo

TRANSLATION INTO ENGLISH

By Kenneth Lyons:

A Traveller's Notes

and: Guadalupe, Zafra, Tordesillas, Pedraza de la Sierra, Olite, Fuente De, Santa María de Huerta, Bayona, Chinchón, El Ferrol, Pontevedra, Zamora, Puerto Lumbreras, Cádiz, Sigüenza, Villacastín.

By Cristopher Robinson:

Viella, Aiguablava, Benicarló, El Saler, Mojacar, Manzanares, Almagro, Granada, Antequera, La Palma, Arcos, Carmona, Cáceres, Salamanca, Tordesillas, Villalba, Gijón, Santillana, Soria, Argomániz, Fuenterrabía and Fuentes Carrionas.

By Giovanna Campesi and Tim Heffernan:

Bielsa, Tortosa, Albacete, La Gomera, Hierro, Mazagón, Jarandilla, Ciudad Rodrigo, Cambados, Ribadeo.

**FROM PARADOR
TO PARADOR
SPAIN**
TOURIST PARADORES

Publication of this book has been possible mainly thanks to the close collaboration of three teams:

The Secretariat General of Tourism,
The Spanish Tourist Administration, A.T.E.
and Luna Wennberg Editores.

Printing was completed at the Luna Wennberg Printing Works, Barcelona.

Luna Wennberg Editores
Barcelona - Madrid
SPAIN